What difference
do it make?

What difference do it make?

Stories of Hope and Healing

RON HALL, DENVER MOORE,
AND LYNN VINCENT

THOMAS NELSON
Since 1798

NASHVILLE   DALLAS   MEXICO CITY   RIO DE JANEIRO

Published in Nashville, Tennessee, by Thomas Nelson. Thomas Nelson is a registered trademark of Thomas Nelson, Inc.

Published in association with the literary agency of Alive Communications, Inc., 7680 Goddard Street, Suite 200, Colorado Springs, CO 80920. www.alivecommunications.com.

Thomas Nelson, Inc. titles may be purchased in bulk for educational, business, fund-raising, or sales promotional use. For information, please e-mail SpecialMarkets@ThomasNelson.com.

Texts of Scripture quoted in this book are taken from the following:

New American Standard Bible®. © The Lockman Foundation 1960, 1962, 1963, 1968, 1971, 1972, 1973, 1975, 1977, 1995. Used by permission:

> John 12:24 (introduction and chapter 12)
> Matthew 25:32–36, 40 (chapter 23)

New King James Version®. © 1982 by Thomas Nelson, Inc. Used by permission. All rights reserved:

> Matthew 10:16 (chapter 25)

Authors paraphrase:

> Matthew 10:24 (chapter 12)
> Matthew 19:26 (chapter 19)
> James 1:22 (chapter 21)

The letter from Vincent Van Gogh, quoted in chapter 9, is excerpted from "Letter from Vincent van Gogh to Theo van Gogh," Cuesmes, July 1880, tr. Mrs. Johanna van Gogh-Bonger, ed. Robert Harrison, number 133, and can be found at WebExhibits, an Interactive Museum, www.webexhibits.org/vangogh/letter/8/133.htm.

Information about homelessness in Sacramento on page 65 is taken from Paul Thompson, "The credit crunch tent city which has returned to haunt America," *Mail Online*, March 6, 2009, www.dailymail.co.uk/news/worldnews/article-1159677/Pictured-The-credit-crunch-tent-city-returned-haunt-America.html (accessed 9 July 2009).

The dialogue between Denver Moore and Mike Daniels, which appears on pages 152–154, was written by Mike Daniels.

ISBN 978-0-8499-4619-6 (trade paper)

Library of Congress Cataloging-in-Publication Data

Hall, Ron, 1945–
    What difference do it make? : stories of hope and healing / Ron Hall, Denver Moore, and Lynn Vincent.
    p. cm.
    ISBN 978-0-8499-2019-6 (hardcover)
    1. Hall, Ron, 1945– 2. Moore, Denver. 3. Hall, Deborah, d. 2000. 4. Whites—Texas—Fort Worth—Biography. 5. African Americans—Texas—Fort Worth—Biography. 6. Homeless men—Texas—Fort Worth—Biography. 7. Indentured servants—Louisiana—Red River Parish—Biography. 8. Art dealers—Texas—Fort Worth—Biography. 9. Christian biography. 10. Fort Worth (Tex.)—Biography. I. Moore, Denver. II. Vincent, Lynn. III. Title.
F394.F7H157 2009
261.8'325092—dc22
[B]
                                        2009029214

Printed in the United States of America

10 11 12 13 14 RRD 5 4 3 2 1

In memory of Debbie,
Denver and Ron dedicate this book to
those who read *Same Kind of Different as Me*
and were inspired to make a difference.

Introduction

*H*ello again.

If you're reading this book, it might be because you already have read *Same Kind of Different as Me*, a true story about my wife, Deborah, and the man who changed our lives, Denver Moore. If you haven't, don't worry—we've included enough of that story to catch you up. (The "catch up" sections from *Same Kind of Different as Me* are in italics.)

Since June 2006, when *Same Kind of Different as Me* snuck first onto bookstore shelves, then onto the *New York Times* bestsellers list, Denver and I have traveled thousands of miles back and forth across America. We've spoken at hundreds of venues, from local book clubs filled with sweet little old ladies to the Bethesda, Maryland, symphony hall. (We were in Bethesda as guests of Doro Bush Koch and her mother, former first lady Barbara Bush, who quite possibly is Denver's biggest fan.) Throughout that time, we have seen thousands of lives changed—homeless shelters started and millions of dollars raised for the homeless, yes, but also astonishing changes in the lives of everyday Americans that we never could've imagined or predicted.

That's why we wrote this book, to tell you just a few of the stories of hope and redemption that God continues to write in the lives of so many—and in our own.

One day in the spring of 2009, as we were writing, I was in the kitchen at the Murchison estate, where Denver and I live, on a conference call with executives at Thomas Nelson, our publisher. During the call, Denver walked in.

"Hey, Denver," I said, putting the call on speaker. "We're talking about titles for the new book. Got any ideas?"

"Title for the new book?" he said, screwing his eyelids down into his famous hard squint. "What difference do it make?"

"*What Difference Do It Make?*" I said. "That's it!"

Denver shrugged and walked off, shaking his head.

It was the perfect title. Since *Same Kind* came out, over and over, like the needle stuck in the groove of an old vinyl record, we've repeated a single message: one person can make a difference. My wife, Deborah Hall, is proof of that.

As many of you know, God took Deborah in 2001. Cancer. But if she were here today, she would tell you she was nobody special. If you had come to our house, she would have made you fresh coffee or tea and invited you to sit down at the kitchen table and tell her about yourself. And you would have felt loved. Because that was Deborah's gift. She loved God and, because of her intimate walk with Him, loved people. Her whole life was about forgiveness and unconditional love, two qualities that most of us find difficult to master on a regular basis.

It really was that simple. Deborah's life showed that kind of love is attainable for anyone willing to put in the time on their knees, then overcome their fear and go out and get their hands a little dirty. And I have talked to literally hundreds of people who told me that Deborah's story inspired them to do just that. Through the difference her life made, others are now making a difference, and that's in part what this book is about. It's packed full with stories folks have shared with us about how Deborah's example inspired them to do more, both in their own homes and in their communities.

A lady named Ann, for example, wrote to us from Vivian, a small Louisiana town just north of Shreveport—not too far from Red River Parish, where Denver worked the plantations. Ann wrote of how she has loaned *Same Kind of Different as Me* to about twenty different friends. Every friend who brings it back has a very different story about how the story affected him or her.

"One person notices the friendship Denver and Ron share," Ann wrote. "Another feels shame over the way her grandparents treated the 'Denvers' in their lives."

One woman surprised Ann by telling her that the portion of

the book that dealt with Deborah's cancer battle stirred her to go and have a colonoscopy she'd been putting off!

Like Ann, we've been struck by the amazing variety of stories people tell us about how Debbie's story affected them. Here we thought we were writing a book about one woman's determination to make a difference for the homeless, and we started getting letters about marriages restored, friendships renewed, ministries begun, even babies adopted!

In Fort Worth, a high school teacher named Carin told us that, "unbelievably," she'd been able to get the school administration to approve our book to be read by her entire mental-health class. "The students have learned how so many issues affect our mental health," Carin wrote. "I have also used the book to help relay to them the importance of community involvement, passion, and what it means to be a servant to others."

Shortly after Deborah died, her best friend, Mary Ellen, told me that God had whispered to her during prayer that Deborah was like the kernel of wheat Jesus refers to in the gospel of John: "Truly, truly, I say to you, unless a grain of wheat falls into the earth and dies, it remains alone; but if it dies, it bears much fruit."

Mary Ellen told me she thought that maybe Deborah's death would be like that—fruitful. I cannot even express how much I absolutely did not want to hear that at the time. But it appears that Mary Ellen was right, more right than even she knew.

She told me about the wheat kernel just a couple of days before the dedication of the Deborah L. Hall Memorial Chapel, the new worship facility built at the Union Gospel Mission in my wife's honor and funded by donations that poured in after local folks heard Denver's story at her memorial service. At the time, we thought the chapel, along with the new care facilities for the homeless, were the fruit God would bring from my wife's death. I had no idea that the Union Gospel Mission was just the *first* fruit in what would become a cornucopia of blessing.

Take Detra, for example. Detra, who lives in Austin, Texas, wrote to tell us that after reading Deborah's story, she decided to start carrying food and socks and blankets in her car so that she can bless the homeless. Also, her church had a picnic in an Austin park and had so much food that they began feeding hungry people who were in the park that day.

One little girl asked Detra, "When are you coming back?"

After that, the church made the picnic a monthly event where church members sit down and break bread with the homeless.

Would I take back blessings like that one and those you are about to read about in this book? If I could rewind time like a video and create a cancer story with a happy ending, would I?

I'm sorry to say there's a big part of me that says, "Yes! I want my wife back!"

But I can tell you without reservation that Deborah would say, "No, Ron. I'll see you soon."

And so the story goes on—men and women all over the country inspired by the story of Denver and Deborah to make a difference in other people's lives. Over the past three years, I thought I was making a difference too—traveling and speaking all over the country, "carrying Miss Debbie's torch," as Denver calls it. And I suppose I was.

But in 2009, I learned that sometimes the most difficult difference to make is the one that's closest to home.

—RON HALL
Dallas, Texas
July 2009

1

Ron

Tennessee sour-mash whiskey defined my daddy. He pledged a lifetime of allegiance to Jim Beam, and ol' Jim never had a more loyal friend. As a boy, tucked into bed in a ratty blue-collar town outside of Fort Worth, I sometimes cried myself to sleep wishing my daddy loved me and my brother, John, as much as he loved Jim.

My father's given name was Earl F. Hall. The F didn't stand for anything, but over the years I assigned it lots of unprintable meanings. Earl was a chain-smoking, chain-drinking ladies' man, who slicked back his wavy brown hair with Vitalis and favored wife-beater T-shirts, pleated gabardine slacks, and wing-tip shoes. He was not a mean drunk and most of the time could walk a straight line and recite the alphabet if he had to. Once he even recited poetry till he sobered up.

When my daddy came home from World War II in '45, we

all lived in his mama's little shack in Denton, Texas, until he could find a job. After a few months he found one working for Curtiss Candy, driving a 1947 GMC panel truck painted red and white like a Baby Ruth wrapper. Not long after that, we piled our meager belongings into the candy truck and moved them over to a one-bedroom bungalow in the West Fourth Street slums near downtown Fort Worth. The neighborhood was planted smack in the geographic center of a shabby circle formed by a rail yard, a hobo camp, a gravel pit, a junkyard, a dog-food factory, and a sewage plant.

Our neighbors were mostly workaday folks, bagging kibble at the plant or spelunking in the sewer lines. Except for Andy, who lived across the street. Andy was a Harley-riding professional wrestler who stayed home all day and wrestled at night. When he wasn't wrestling in the ring, he wrestled naked in his living room with his redheaded bombshell wife, Rusty Fay. For some reason Rusty Fay had never gotten around to hanging curtains in the front room, so the picture window that faced our street drew neighborhood boys like the hootchy-cootchy tent at an old-time carnival. We never could figure out how little Rusty Fay always managed to pin her big, brawny husband and wind up on top, but we all thought it was the best show in town.

From a boy's perspective, that was about the only thing my neighborhood had going for it. For one thing, the place stunk to high heaven. Smelly emissions from the sewage facility and the dog-food plant settled in the trees like an invisible fog with a combined scent that reminded me of a roomful of old men after a chili cook-off. Those fumes competed with equally unpleasant ones from hobo campfires, backyard chicken droppings, and the working outhouse that our next-door neighbors kept out back. Once, on a school field trip, I smelled the warm, cinnamon scent of a bakery and was jealous of any kids fortunate enough to live nearby.

Our house sat near a rail yard with acres of tracks planted like row crops that produced a year-round yield of multicolored boxcars and a round-the-clock clang of crossing bells. Day and night, the cars collided in a steady, drum-like rhythm as screeching engines slammed them together to form mile-long strings that chugged out of the yard with hobos in hot pursuit. (The good news about the rail yard was that my friends and I, through many scientific trials, disproved the old wives' tale that a single penny on the tracks can derail a moving train.)

Playing second fiddle to the rail-yard symphony were the grain elevators and the dog-food plant, each of which produced an uninterrupted, high-pitched whine. But none of these noises was as obnoxious or caustic as my parents' constant fighting.

I have heard it said that a thin line exists between love and hate. From the epithets I often heard floating through the open windows into the front yard, I thought Earl and Tommye Hall were hell-bent on erasing the line entirely.

Most of their screaming matches took place in mornings and afternoons since most nights Daddy hid out at the Tailless

Monkey Bar. Then, just before midnight, he'd call home and make Mama come and get him. She'd wake us up and drive the mile or so to the Tailless Monkey. She'd honk, and he'd stumble out. After we were old enough to walk and talk, John and I would fight until the loser had to go in and get him. Earl would usually be sitting with his buddies at a table, sometimes with a woman on his lap. Daddy was handsome and attracted the barflies like ants to a family picnic.

"Gimme some sugar," he would slur, trying to kiss me on the mouth. I'd wiggle out of his grip and turn my head because I hated the way beer and smoke smelled on his breath.

Daddy didn't set out to destroy me, and I didn't let him, though there was no avoiding his influence. I promised myself I'd never drink or smoke, and I managed to make it to age five before I started smoking grapevine and age six before I started smoking Kool menthols stolen from Elizabeth Henson's daddy, who drove a dump truck for the neighborhood gravel pit. I had my first drink, a Pabst Blue Ribbon, at the age of fourteen. It is sometimes a sad irony of boyhood that sons can emulate their fathers and simultaneously loathe them.

2

Denver

otta times, people look at homeless folks the way they used
to look at me: they'd kinda eyeball me up and down, and I
could see them wheels turnin in their heads, wonderin, how'd
that fella get that way?

See, that ain't the right question to be askin 'cause it might
be that ain't none a' our business. Our business is to find out is
there anything we can do to bring a change in their life. To bring
opportunity. To bring hope. Sometimes that might mean gettin
a man off liquor or drugs. It might mean helpin him find a job.

Here's my story. When I showed up in Fort Worth, Texas, I
couldn't read, couldn't write, and couldn't do a lick a' rithmetic. I
had growed up on a plantation in the Deep South and never went
to school a day in my life.

I was born in Red River Parish, Louisiana, in 1937, a time
when whites was white and blacks was "colored." Officially, there

wadn't no slavery, but that didn't mean there wadn't no slaves. All around the South we had what we called sharecroppers. Now, my daddy, BB, wadn't no sharecropper. He was a railroad worker, I think—I never did know for sure—and a ladies' man that couldn't set foot in the New Mary Magdelene Baptist Church on Sundays 'cause he'd been steppin out with some of the women in the congregation. But BB got stabbed to death one night in Grand Bayou right out there by Highway 1. My grandma, Big Mama, had already burned up in a house fire by then, and me and brother, Thurman, went to live with my Aunt Etha and Uncle James. They was sharecroppin on a plantation down there near Coushatta.

When you is croppin, here's how it works. The Man that own the plantation give you everthing you need to make a cotton crop, 'cept he give it to you on credit. Then you plant and plow and chop that cotton till pickin time. And when you bring in that cotton, you s'posed to split that crop down the middle, or maybe 60/40, and the Man take his share and you take yours. 'Cept somehow it never did work out that way 'cause by the time you pay the man back for all he done loaned you on credit, ain't nothin left outta your share a' the crop. In fact, most a' the time, you in the hole, so you got to work another season on the plantation to pay back what you owe.

From the time I was a little-bitty boy, I was a cropper. Didn't know how to do nothin 'cept plantation work—plowin, plantin, choppin, pickin, and whatever odd jobs there was to do, like tryin to nail scrap boards in the floor of the shack the Man let us live in.

I worked like that all the way till the 1960s, all without no paycheck. Then one day when I was grown, I realized I wadn't never gon' get ahead. I wadn't *never* gon' be able to pay the Man back what I owed. So I hopped on a freight train that come runnin through the country and wound up in Fort Worth, Texas. Even though I hadn't ever been outta Red River Parish, I'd heard there was plenty a' work in the cities. But once I got there, I found out there wadn't too many folks willin to hire a colored fella who couldn't read, couldn't write, and couldn't figure.

I got me a few odd jobs here and there, but it wadn't enough to pay for a place to live. So I wound up homeless.

Now, let's say you walked up to me on East Lancaster Street in Fort Worth and asked me, said, why you homeless? Why you down on your luck?

If I told you about BB and Big Mama and the Man, if I told you that I used to work plantations like a slave almost up until the time America put a man on the moon, what you gon' say?

"Here's a dollar"?

"Good luck and God bless"?

A lotta homeless folks has been hurt and abused since we was little bitty. At one time or another we loved or was loved by somebody. We had hope. We believed. Then hope flew out the door, and everthing we had was gone. For a lot of us there come a time when nobody was willin to take us in. Nobody was willin to help in no kinda way. All the doors was slammed in our faces, and next thing you know, we just sittin on the curb with everbody passin us by, won't even look at us.

Even though you is still a human bein inside, even though you mighta been a little boy once with a mama, even though you mighta been married once with a house and a job, now you ain't nothin. And once that happens, people rather come up and pet a stray dog than even say hello.

Sometimes we becomes homeless 'cause we done some real bad thing, somethin so bad that everbody in our life just stop lovin and trustin us. And when you ain't got no one to love you and trust you, you becomes like a wild animal, hidin and livin in the dark. Even when you see them homeless fellas on the street that look real cheerful and happy, that's just a mask. Underneath is a swamp of misery, but they puttin on that mask so they can get through the day. Maybe scare up a dollar or two so they can get somethin to eat or a half-pint to take the edge off the pain.

No, if you'd a' seen me back then, you prob'ly wouldn'ta believed my story. You mighta even just rolled on by and said to yourself, "Idle hands is the devil's workshop! Why don't that lazy fella get a job?"

LUCY

Love in a Ziploc Bag

"Mama, who is that brown man?"

When seven-year-old Lucy Barnes went to bed the night before, her mama had been sitting in an overstuffed chair, reading a book. When Lucy woke up, her mama was tucked into the same chair with the same book. Now Lucy wanted to know about the man on the cover.

"His name is Denver, and he is a homeless man," Reta Barnes said.

A puzzled look furrowed Lucy's small face. "What's homeless?"

A little embarrassed, Reta suddenly realized she had never explained homelessness to her daughter. It wasn't that she was sheltering Lucy. It was just that the subject had never come up. In their tiny town of Fairhope, Alabama, she had never seen anyone sleeping on the streets. Later that year, we would read about Lucy in an Alabama newspaper. But on that morning she was just a little girl asking questions.

Reta looked at her daughter and tried to keep her explanation simple.

"There are men and women and children who don't have homes," Reta said as Lucy peered at her with serious eyes.

"They don't have food, they don't have jobs, and they can't afford homes. So they find the best place they can to sleep, maybe under a bridge or on a park bench. They sleep with their coats over them and make do with what they have."

Lucy reflected on this for a moment. Then she said, "Why can't they just get a job?"

Reta paused. She knew that some homeless people *could* get jobs but didn't want to. But that would confuse the issue beyond the capacity of a seven-year-old. Reta decided to teach her daughter about the truly needy.

"Some homeless people who can't get jobs are women who don't have any place to leave their children," Reta said. "Some can't get jobs because they're sick. Some lost their homes because they were out of work, and now they can't get a job because they have to keep moving around to find a place to sleep."

Then Reta explained that there are places called rescue missions where homeless people can go to get help. "There's one right across the bay in Mobile," she said.

Lucy Barnes did not ooh and aah or receive this information with wide eyes. She just took it all in. But the next thing Reta knew, Lucy had gone to every member of her family and hit them up for cash.

"I'm raising money for the homeless!" she would say cheerfully. She even braced her grandmother, who lives in a nursing home.

A couple of days later, Lucy popped into the kitchen where her mother was fixing lunch. "Can I have a lemonade stand?" the little girl asked.

A half hour later, armed with a pitcher of Crystal Light lemonade and a homemade sign, Lucy started flagging down folks driving through her neighborhood while Reta looked on from a folding camp chair.

Lucy kept up her pitch: "I'm raising money for the homeless!" She was charging twenty-five cents a cup, but her customers always threw in a little extra since it was for a good cause.

By the end of the afternoon, Lucy's impromptu enterprise had added a few dollars to her fund, and Reta thought that was probably that. But Lucy wasn't finished yet. The next day, she and two young friends went door-to-door in her neighborhood, repeating Lucy's now-familiar refrain: "We're raising money for the homeless!"

One family thrilled the girls when they chipped in twenty dollars in one whack. "We were, like, whoa! That's so cool!" Lucy remembers.

Reta Barnes, meanwhile, observed her daughter's philanthropy with amazement. No one had suggested to Lucy that she do any of this fund-raising. She did it all on her own. Reta thought her little girl was setting a very grown-up example.

Between her family, neighbors, and lemonade customers, Lucy had raised a little under ninety dollars. At first, she wanted to take the whole sum and deliver it to one homeless person. But Reta suggested an alternative. Maybe they should take the money to the rescue mission in Mobile. "The people there will know how best to use the money to help the homeless."

Lucy thought that was a good idea, so her mother called Carrie, the volunteer coordinator at the mission, and set a date to visit a couple of weeks in the future.

The day before the trip, the telephone rang at the Barnes home. It was Miss Lott, Lucy's second-grade teacher. "Reta, I just wanted you to know that Lucy has written a letter to her classmates saying she's going to the rescue mission," Miss Lott said. "She told the other kids that if any of them have any money or clothes they want to donate, she'll be happy to take it to the rescue mission when she goes."

Once again, Reta was astonished. She had thought Lucy's fund-raising drive was over. But then, without fanfare, Lucy just kept going. The morning of the mission trip, some of her classmates brought clothes from home, along with a few dollars, for Lucy to take to the mission. And so that all the children could participate in the giving, Miss Lott broke a twenty-dollar bill into singles and let each student contribute a dollar.

Reta was amazed at the chain reaction caused by her daughter's initiative. Lucy's small acts of determined kindness were like stones in a pond, the ripples spreading out to her family, neighbors, and classmates, even her teacher. By the day of the mission trip in May 2008, Lucy had raised $113 in coins and cash, including one very exciting twenty-dollar bill. She proudly tucked her treasure into a Ziploc bag. Until that day, she had never even seen a homeless person. But that day, she toured the mission and even helped serve a meal.

"I saw a lot of brown men, like Denver on the book cover," she remembers. "It was really fun because I got to give them fruit!"

She also got to give Carrie, the volunteer coordinator, the Ziploc bag filled with money. Inside the bag, Lucy had tucked a note for the homeless:

I love you, and God does too.

3

Ron

Daddy started out a comical, fun-loving man who retired from Coca-Cola after forty-odd years of service. But somewhere during my childhood, he crawled into a whiskey bottle and didn't come out till I was grown.

My daddy, Earl, was raised by a single mother, Clarabell, and two old-maid aunts, Edna and Florence. None of them ever drove a car; they walked to their jobs as maids at the laundry for the Southern Hotel and the Texas State College for Women. Their little house never saw a coat of paint inside or out. They had no telephone, heated the place with a four-burner kitchen stove that I never in my life saw turned off, and considered air-conditioning a dream on par with someday owning an estate like John D. and Lupe Murchison, the richest people in Texas.

Mama Clara and Aunt Edna and Aunt Florence dipped

Garrett snuff. Between the three sisters, they went through a whole jar of it every day. The smell was nauseating, and it ran down their chins and dried deep in the wrinkles. I would rather have had a leather belt whipping than kiss one of them. But once a month, when we visited the three sisters in their little shack across the tracks in Denton, Daddy made me say hello and good-bye with a kiss on the mouth. I squinched my eyes shut, made my lips as thin as I could, and endured it. Maybe Edna and Florence knew it was a trial for me because they always gave me a jar of pennies as a kind of reward.

But they were mighty sweet, and Son, as they called Daddy, was all they had.

My grandmother, Clarabell, wore the shame of being a single mother like a leper. She seldom made eye contact with anyone but her sisters. I recently read a book about single mothers, *Holding Her Head High*, by the actress Janine Turner. I wish Mama Clara could have read it and held hers high, but I don't believe she could read, and because of her shame, her chin always rested on her chest.

When he was seven years old, Daddy had to go to work to help make ends meet. He wound up washing bottles in a 7-Up plant. Mama Clara and the aunties strictly forbade him to ask for any information about his father. Later, when I came along, the don't-ask-don't-tell policy was still in force.

I remember sitting on the front stoop with Aunt Edna and Aunt Florence one day when I was about eight, each aunt with her little lump of Garrett causing her lower lip to poke out like a permanent pout. With the Texas sun heating up the porch and the seat of my dungarees, I was feeling a little brave.

"Tell me a story about my granddaddy," I ventured.

The sisters barked in unison, "You don't have one!" Then Edna turned her head and spit in the yard.

As I got older, I realized it couldn't be true that my daddy didn't have a daddy, as there was only one virgin birth ever recorded. Once, my brother, John, told me he thought Aunt Edna was our grandfather.

In any case, all his life, when Daddy asked who his father was, the sisters gave him the same answer. Finally, when he shipped off to fight the war in the Pacific in 1942, he quit asking. He was seventy-five years old when his mother died. Florence, the oldest aunt, was on her deathbed when she told him his father was named Wanda and that he was from Stephenville, Texas. But it was too late to go looking for him, even though there could not have been another man named Wanda in all of Texas.

My mama raised us like a single mom with no help from Earl. As opposed to Mama Clara, she held her head high, leading by example. She taught us the Bible and dragged us off to Sunday school and church every week—no excuses, no absences unless one of us was broken out with chicken pox or measles.

Not even circumcision was an excuse. When my brother was five, he got circumcised on a Friday and bled like a stuck hog. On Sunday morning he was no better, so Mama wrapped his penis in a sock, looped Scotch tape around the package three or four times, and hauled us off to church. Sitting on the front pew, I was too scared to ask to go to the bathroom for fear of what other creative uses my mama could find for tape and a sock. So I just sat there and pooped in my pants.

I never remember my daddy ever setting foot in church, except once or twice on Easter when I was in junior high and high school. I don't have a clue what he did on Sundays when the Monkey was closed, but we never saw him. In fact, I can't remember him ever driving us anywhere, except when he moved us to the slums in the candy truck. Sometimes he would go with us when we went somewhere, but my mother was always the designated driver so he could be the designated drinker.

Mama taught us how to throw a baseball, and she also helped coach our games. We'd drop Daddy off at the Monkey before the games and pick him up after.

"Paste that ol' pill!" he'd command as the door slammed on our '49 Pontiac. What he really meant was, "Hit the ball." Later he'd ask, "Did you paste that ol' pill for your daddy?"

That was Earl Hall's definition of involved fatherhood.

My mama, Tommye, was a farm girl from Barry, Texas, who sewed every stitch of clothing we wore, baked cookies, and cheered me on at Little League . . . Tommye, [her brother] Buddy, [and her sisters] Elvice and . . . Vida May . . . all picked cotton on the blackland farm owned by their daddy and my granddaddy, Mr. Jack Brooks.

We were poor but not the charity kind. My mama, Tommye, was a resourceful old farm gal who raised chickens in the backyard and sold the excess eggs and roosters to the neighbors. We always had plenty to eat, a rich diet of yard bird, fried Spam, and Van Camp's pork and beans. Mama bought those beans by the case and stored them in the garage like she was preparing for Y2K. Our daily dose of them produced indoor smells to rival those indigenous to the neighborhood. Daddy always tried to blame the smell of his farts on the neighbor's outhouse. But when I messed in my britches that time at church and tried the same thing, Mama said we were more than a mile away from there and not to be acting like my daddy.

My parents slept on a fold-out sofa in the living room of our tiny asphalt-shingled bungalow. Outside we had a dirt yard. The dirt was smooth and powder-fine, perfect for playing with a toy dump truck—except we didn't have one. Still, our little place looked downright fancy compared to the tar-paper shacks and unpainted lean-tos that perched precariously on bois d'arc stumps around the gravel pit nearby. The kids who lived in those sad-looking homes were even lower on the social totem pole than we were, dirty little ragamuffins who depended on handouts and sometimes had to scrounge in the trash. I heard their daddies were mostly former employees of the gravel company.

At least they have daddies, I thought. John and I may have been living higher on the hog than the gravel-pit kids, but I would have traded places with them to have a real daddy.

Once, we took a vacation to Monterrey, Mexico, because Daddy had heard American tourists there could drink free Carta Blanca beer all day long. At Earl's insistence, my mother drove for two days straight through, across the Texas and Mexican deserts in a four-door '49 Pontiac sedan, so that he could drink free in the beer garden at the Carta Blanca Brewery. That was years before air-conditioning was an option.

We'd drop Daddy off at the brewery in the morning, and John and I would swim all day at a semipublic pool near our cheap tourist court. Mama didn't know how to swim, so she just sat in a chair, never taking her eyes off us and holding a life preserver just in case. Right at closing time, we'd pick Daddy up.

The whole "free Carta Blanca" thing was a real losing proposition for the company because Earl Hall never drank that brand at home. In fact, his buddies at the Monkey called him "Earl the Pearl" because he always had his fingers wrapped around a cold can of Pearl beer. He loved to show off how he could crush the cans with one bare hand. That was long before the days of aluminum, when Alcoa steel cans ruled.

Once when John was in the seventh grade, the junior high was having a donkey basketball game. In case you never saw one, the fathers rode donkeys and played against the sons. John was tall and had made the basketball team.

Somehow, he convinced our dad that all fathers were required to ride. Dad got home early that day, and with the help of a pint of his buddy Jim Beam, he mustered up the courage to crawl up on a donkey.

Things went pretty well the first few times the donkeys ran back and forth down the court in a smooth gait like a Tennessee walking horse. Dad made a pass or two and attempted to block John's shot. Then something went terribly wrong. Dad's donkey got a burr under its saddle and launched him like an astronaut. After a back flip with a double twist, he landed on his elbow, crushing it like an empty Pearl can. I'm sure it was painful because I think Dad was crying, but John and I laughed our butts off. That was the most fun we ever had with him.

I can't remember whether he came to any of my high school or college graduations . . . but probably not. By then, I was glad he didn't show up because he was a stranger whose only purpose, as far as I was concerned, was to embarrass me.

But other folks didn't feel that way about Earl at all. He was well liked by his employer and associates, who appreciated his wit and his don't-give-a-crap attitude. His buddies said he was as funny as Jackie Gleason and laughed from the gut every time he started spinning a tall tale. They guffawed especially loud went Earl went on a tear about the Republicans.

"Them damn Republicans are responsible for everything bad in the whole world," Daddy'd holler like he was speaking through a bullhorn from the back of a rail car on a whistle-stop campaign tour. He blamed the GOP for everything from communism to arthritis. And if he temporarily ran out of things to blame them for, he might throw in acne and ingrown toenails.

The whole time Dwight D. Eisenhower was in the White House, Daddy thought Texas senator Lyndon B. Johnson was a sterling hero who could save America and ought to kick Ike out on his can. When John F. Kennedy ran in 1960, Daddy didn't much like him. But Earl was a yellow-dog Democrat who would vote for a four-legged canine of any color before he would vote for a Republican. So when November came, he held his nose and voted for JFK, even if the man was a Catholic and a Yankee.

4

Denver

Ever Sunday, a field hand drivin a mule wagon wound down the dirt plantation road gatherin up colored folks to haul em off to praise the Lord . . . The preacher, Brother Eustis Brown, was just another field hand. But he was the onlyest man I knowed besides [my] Uncle James that could read the Bible . . .

"Brother Brown, we done heard that message about a hun'erd times," one of the older women would say, somebody with gumption like my auntie, Big Mama's sister. "When you gon' change the sermon?"

Brother Brown would just gaze up at the [church's] holey roof and shake his head, kinda sad. "I work out there in the cotton with y'all, and ever week, the Lord shows me what's goin on in the congregation so I'll know what to preach on Sunday. When I start seein some changes out there," he'd say, pointing toward the plantation, "I'll be changin what I preach in here."

That's how I learned the Bible without knowin how to read.

Aunt Etha and Uncle James didn't have a single book in their shotgun shack 'cept the Bible. I didn't know how to read it, though, 'cause at that time colored children couldn't go to school. I had heard of some colored children gettin some schoolin in some other places, but on my plantation in Red River Parish, we stayed home and worked the fields. There was one time when all the children worked, white and colored, and that was pickin time. When King Cotton came in, *all* the kids stayed home and helped.

After we worked in the fields, the white kids would go inside their houses and get cleaned up for supper. But the colored kids would line up on the front porch, every one of us naked as a jay-bird, to take our bath in a number-ten washtub. We all used the same water 'cause the water come from a cistern that catched the rain off the roof, and we didn't have no water to throw away. We had some well water, too, from a well that I had watched three or four sharecroppers dig. But that water was as cold as snow. Wadn't no way we wanted to take a bath in that.

When I was a teenager, I started to earn a few pennies here and there scrappin cotton for the Man. There wadn't no place to spend it 'cept at the Man's store on the plantation, but I saved it anyway in a Prince Albert tobacco can with a hole cut in the top.

I hid that can in the crawl space underneath Aunt Etha's house, and I remember one time when we was gon' go into town, I was real happy 'cause we hardly ever went to town. Now I was gon' get to spend my pennies in a real store, not the Man's store. But when I went up under the house to get the money, I detected a crime. The Prince Albert can was still there, but it was stone-cold empty!

For a coupla minutes, I just hunkered there down under the floorboards with the dirt and the spiders, thinkin. After a while, I recollected a clue. Sometimes I had seen my brother, Thurman, walkin down the red plantation road eatin some candy or some cheese that he got. A coupla times, he had some cheese in his mouth and a stick a' candy pokin out the pocket of his overalls like he was some kinda rich fella livin high on the hog. And now I remembered he wouldn't give me none of it, and he wouldn't tell me how he got it neither.

Well, once I recollected that, I figured out that the money thief couldn'ta been nobody but Thurman, and I was sho 'nough *peeved off.*

I stormed up out from under the house, hollerin, "Thurman! Thurman stole my money!"

Well, Thurman must a' heard me 'cause right then he come bustin through the front door of Aunt Etha's, runnin like somebody'd set his feet on fire. Burnin mad, I picked up an old brick and chased my brother 'round an' 'round the outside of the house like we was wooden horses on a merry-go-round.

But he was older than me and a little faster, and I never could catch him. So I got smart and stopped by the corner near the cistern and waited. Things got real quiet, and I couldn't hear Thurman runnin no more.

"Li'l Buddy?" he called out. That's what everbody called me then.

I kept my mouth shut, quiet as a squirrel hidin from a bobcat.

Right then, Thurman stuck his ugly head out from around the corner of the house, and I let that brick go flyin.

Bull's-eye! Hit him square upside the head!

I was mighty proud a' standin up for myself. Thurman wobbled like a drunk man, and I even drew blood. But Uncle James wadn't proud at all, and he gave me the worst whuppin of my life.

From that time on, I was discouraged 'bout trustin folks, even the ones you s'posed to be able to trust, like your brother.

5

Ron

*The first time I saw Deborah, I began plotting to steal her.
Not for myself at first, but for Sigma Chi, the fraternity I
pledged after transferring from East Texas State to [Texas
Christian University] . . . It was the spring of 1965, and I
was on academic probation. Deborah, meanwhile, was a soph-
omore on an academic scholarship . . . I planned to make her
a Sigma Chi sweetheart, a little inter-frat coup that carried
with it the novel perk of adding an intellectual girl to our
table at the Student Union.*

In the spring of 1969, I asked Deborah to marry me. Early
on, we discovered that we were not able to have children the
old-fashioned way, though trying was an awful lot of fun.

When we told my daddy that we were unable to have children, he questioned my manhood. When we told him we had

put our names on the list at the Edna Gladney Home to adopt two children, his face turned grim, and he pointed an index finger in my face: "That's a real big mistake, Buddy-roo," he said. "You'll be sorry."

Earl Hall was against adoption and in favor of orphan homes and prison. In his opinion, there was no way in hell a person would give up a child for adoption unless that child was going to be, to use his words, "ugly or a retard."

To his way of thinking, there was a good chance of our winding up with a child who was both.

Thankfully, he lived to eat those words as God blessed us with Regan and Carson, who we believed were perfect little babes who had been tucked under dewy leaves in the garden of Eden, just waiting for us and meant to be ours.

Daddy never once called them or came to see them. (At least he was consistent.) But we took the kids to see him, and they loved and honored him in spite of himself.

ABE

The Ripple Effect

It took a few years, but Emily Alexander has learned never to say never. We heard about Emily and her husband, Moody, through their friend Mandy Elmore, another *Same Kind* reader. (Mandy has her own story, which you can read about beginning on page *118*.)

Married for fifteen years, the Alexanders, who live just down the road from us in Arlington, Texas, intentionally built themselves a good-sized family. Their oldest son, Hill, was born thirteen years ago. Then they had Wick, another son, now eleven, followed by daughter Avery, now ten, and little Isabelle, seven, whom they call Issy for short.

And that was that.

When people would ask Emily whether she was done having kids, she wouldn't just say yes. She'd say, "Done, done, *done*! Four is enough!"

"We were content with our family size and felt fulfilled," Moody says, adding that he had taken medical steps to keep it that way.

But then Emily also said she'd never homeschool—and she started homeschooling Hill at age six. "The Lord often has a plan far different from our own," she says.

In early 2007, Emily read *Same Kind of Different as Me;* then she passed it on to Moody. Both of them felt what she calls a "proper unsettling," a sense of no longer being content with the status quo. "I remember calling my sister and telling her that I was afraid of having regrets, of getting to the end of my life and knowing I could've done more to make a difference—but didn't."

Emily and Moody began praying, searching for a place to make that difference, a way to help. "I thought maybe it would involve driving right down the road and helping out at the Union Gospel Mission in Fort Worth," Emily says.

Instead, the Alexander grown-ups found the answer right under their own roof.

The Alexander kids had never cottoned to their parents' idea that four kids was enough. Over the years, they'd clamored for more siblings, reminding Emily and Alexander how much *fun* it would be to have a baby around the house. Especially Avery, who absolutely adored babies and wanted one of her own to care for. Even Moody's medical guarantee against a bigger family proved no obstacle for the Alexander kids, who lobbied for adoption on a regular basis.

Later in 2007, one of Emily's college friends, a woman named Kristin, went on a summer mission trip to Zambia. Excited for their friend and still searching for some larger purpose in life, the Alexanders sat down to watch a DVD about the mission. The video featured dark-skinned, chocolate-eyed children with faces like cherubs . . . and with no parents. Kristin was going to work in an orphanage.

Little Isabelle spoke up immediately. "Why can't we just bring one of those kids home?"

"No," Emily told her. "We feel like our family's complete."

The children pointed out that some family friends of the Alexanders had adopted children from Africa.

"Well, that's so great for them," Emily said, smiling. "But I don't think that's what God has in mind for our family."

Then Hill, the oldest boy, said to his mother, "Well, will you at least please pray about it?"

And what do you say to that but yes?

A series of circumstances and events—the kids' longing, the tugging on their own hearts when they saw the plight of African children, and their own search for a larger purpose—convinced the Alexanders to take the adoption plunge. A little research showed them that even though twenty-five million orphans live in Africa, Ethiopia is one of just a handful of African nations that allow international adoptions. And most of the time, Ethiopian children are adopted by twos, threes, and fours since it is the government's policy not to split up siblings.

So it was settled. The Alexanders would apply to adopt an Ethiopian child—and not just one child but two.

"We actually liked the idea of adopting two children,"

Moody said of the children they hoped would become part of their family. "We thought it would help with the transition. Plus, our kids couldn't decide between a little brother and a little sister!"

So Emily and Moody requested a brother/sister set between the ages of one and five.

The Alexanders began saving money for a family trip to Ethiopia to take place in the summer of 2008, and the kids were overjoyed. But Avery, who was eight years old at the time, was not about to let either her parents or the Ethiopian government decide she was going to have just a *little* brother and sister. She wanted a *baby*.

B-a-b-y.

One day, while feeding a bottle to the adopted baby of Alexander family friends, a little boy named Silas, Avery began to cry. She told Emily that she wanted a *baby* from Africa, not a toddler—or worse, somebody already well on his or her way to being a big kid.

But Emily didn't want Avery to be under any delusions. "I continually reminded her that we wouldn't be receiving a referral of an infant," she says. "I knew where we were on the wait list, and I knew several families ahead of us who were specifically requesting infants in their sibling groups."

Emily gently told Avery not to get her hopes up.

Avery walked away, telling Emily over her shoulder, "Well, I can still *pray* for a baby."

In May 2008, the Alexanders received amazing news. Adoption officials in Ethiopia referred to the family a two-month old baby boy.

"Here's the baby you prayed for," Emily said when she placed the baby in Avery's arms.

The Alexanders' story doesn't end there. After caring for Abe for several weeks, the family noticed that the baby seemed developmentally delayed. He wasn't sitting up yet, had zero head control, and didn't seem to have a normal range of movement for a child his age. At first the Alexanders chalked the problems up to the lack of nurturing a child would receive in a nuclear family. But soon they suspected it was something more.

After an extensive series of medical tests, doctors delivered their diagnosis. It appeared Abe had suffered several strokes inside the womb. The baby had a form of cerebral palsy. Worse, his brain was missing its entire frontal lobe.

"The day we got Abe's diagnosis, we were devastated," Emily remembers. She and Moody had to work hard not to allow their minds to wander off into worst-case scenarios. Still, Emily cried over what she felt in some ways was a broken dream.

But little Avery held the dream up in a new light. She had spent hours with construction paper and glue, creating a collage composed of pictures of her new baby brother, especially pictures of Avery and Abe together. Also, she painstakingly

cut individual letters out of magazine headlines to create a
title for her artwork:

For This Child I Prayed

When Emily saw Avery's finished project, she read the title
out loud—"For *this* child I prayed"—and realized that there
was nothing accidental or broken about Abe's presence in
the Alexander family.

"I got to a point pretty quickly after his diagnosis that of
every mom in the world, God chose *me* to be Abe's mom,"
Emily remembers. "The Lord has given me an incredible
amount of patience. For example, Abe doesn't sleep, so I
don't sleep. But things that at one point seemed like a big
deal just aren't a big deal anymore. Abe has simplified our
lives in the best way."

Had he stayed in Ethiopia, Abe would not have survived.
But here, in America, he is making so much progress that
neurologists say he is literally defying modern medicine.
Responses that would normally travel through the frontal
lobe seem to have found a back road in Abe's brain.

"He's super alert," Emily said. "He tracks with his eyes,
has great facial recognition, and he can hear and verbalize."

One doctor told the Alexanders, "If I hadn't seen Abe before
I saw his MRI, I would never think it was the same child."

By April 2009, during occupational therapy sessions,

Abe was beginning to be able to move his left leg and arm, creating new neurological connections and confirming for his amazed family that God was at work.

"[Abe] was super determined and not nearly as miserable as some of the faces he managed to make," Emily wrote on the family's blog. "Keep praying—we *see* Him working daily."

Everyone is so quick to say that Abe is blessed that a family like the Alexanders adopted him, Emily says. "But our family is so much more blessed to have Abe. He is this fourteen-month-old teacher. Sometimes just opening his hand takes an enormous amount of effort and energy, but Abe works so hard in therapy, and my other kids get to see this determination. He just has this little, bright light, radiating an inner joy that you can't explain."

The Alexanders like to talk about "the ripple effect" of Abe's adoption. Like throwing a pebble in a pond, it has brought people together who have gone on the journey with them, both physically and spiritually. Through Abe, the Alexander children have learned to pray more consistently and more specifically, and they have passed that lesson along to others. A young boy named Jeremiah, the son of family friends, called to say there is a tree near his home that blooms red in winter and reminds him of Abe. Jeremiah prays for Abe every day when he passes the tree on his way to school. In May 2009, the Alexanders received an e-mail from dear friends who said that after watching Abe and his new family, they, too, have decided to adopt a child. The same month, the Alexanders completed their paperwork for a second adoption from Ethiopia.

6

Ron

Every couple of months, Deborah and I would take Mama and Daddy to a nice restaurant. He would grab the first waitress he laid eyes on, whether ours or not, and in a voice much louder than necessary, say, "Honey, before you do another thing, I need a whiskey—Jim Beam and Coke, not too much Coke!"

I remember one night at a restaurant when I'd had enough of his disrespecting my mama, and I let a disgusted look creep onto my face. He looked back at me, puzzled, as though I were an alien specimen from an unknown universe.

"What have you got against drinking?" he said, sure that had to be the problem.

"Nothing, Dad. Sometimes I even have one."

"Well then, why won't you drink with your old daddy? You think you're too good?"

Never did I let him see me take a drink. I even quit drinking altogether for a couple of years. That was after Carson, who was an otherwise perfect child, came home drunk in high school and wrecked his room with a boat paddle from Kanakuk Christian camp. When I was sure I never craved alcohol, I started again, allowing myself wine with a fancy dinner.

By 1975, I was working in investment banking in Fort Worth, where I first made my mark as a fine-arts dealer. I quickly got too big for my britches and, in 1986, decided we needed to move to Dallas in order to grow my business and be truly appreciated by the art-world elite.

That's where Deborah and I started to grow apart. While I stormed the art world and collected a closetful of Armani suits and custom-made boots painstakingly handmade from the skins of various animals, Deborah plugged into God, pursuing a passionate spiritual life that included working with AIDS babies and hours spent on her knees in prayer.

Those were sometimes lonely days for Deborah. In Dallas, she had a tough time finding friends who were willing to venture deep into spiritual waters. Most people (including me) were happy to watch from the shore. Some braved the shallow end on occasion, but most were afraid of getting in over their heads.

When we first arrived in town, Deborah wanted to pray for our children, Regan and Carson, and all their classmates and the teachers in the school, so she started a weekly prayer group and invited all the mothers in Carson's grade. I remember how puzzled Deborah was that several women in our neighborhood seemed hesitant about the invitation. Many times, nobody showed up at all.

"Why would anyone *not* want to pray over their kids?" she asked me one day.

Later, I heard through the grapevine that most people were a little afraid of Deborah's intimacy with God. They were especially afraid because she invited them to do the scariest thing of all: pray with her *out loud*.

To tell you the truth, even I felt intimidated when praying with her. Deborah prayed with such passion—not like some nut-ball holy roller but with such knowledge of the Father as though He was her daddy and she was His favorite child. Without pausing or stumbling, she let her words flow like a psalm or a sonnet. Captured on canvas, her prayers would be considered masterpieces, like a Rubens or a Caravaggio. And yet her prayers were not *artful*, as though she meant to impress. Instead, she would simply remind God of His own promises in Scripture and, in an inexplicably reverent way, sort of shake Him by His lapels when she thought He really ought to get moving on a particular project.

There was a depth, an intensity, a beauty to my wife's prayers, as if she had boldly stepped into a rare inner circle of divine light that others dared only regard from a distance. And in the beginning, that irritated me. It was as if she was so spiritual that she wasn't being real or down-to-earth. So I understood why the ladies didn't want to show up and secretly wished I had that option.

Before long, Deborah and I had grown so far apart that I was looking for a way out. She was sure I loved art and money but not so sure I loved her. I knew she loved God and our kids but was fairly certain she could just barely stand the sight of me. And so, in 1988, when I found myself in Beverly Hills, sharing wine with a beautiful blonde painter, I made a lot of excuses to myself on the way to a hotel room.

After a friend threatened to rat me out, I confessed. Deborah and I went to marriage counseling, and she forgave me. She also told me a truth about women's hearts that I wish I could tattoo on the insides of every married man's eyelids: "I know you're an art dealer and that you love ranches and horses and longhorn steers and fancy cars. But what I don't know about you is what's in your heart. What you're thinking when you look at me, when you hold me. Even if you're thinking you don't like me very much at that moment, I can deal with that. What I can't deal with is not knowing your heart."

Of course, that scared the crap out of me. Every man reading this knows his heart is a place so dangerous not even he feels safe going there. But I also knew that as much as I yearned to know my wife on an intimate physical level, she yearned for emotional and spiritual intimacy. Suddenly, I understood that just as sex—lots of it—was important to me, *knowing* me, *experiencing* my interior world, was important to her.

From then on, Deborah and I prayed together, usually lying together in bed. I would hold her in my arms, and she would know my heart according to my prayers. At first, I prayed about things I thought she'd want me to pray about: our marriage, the kids, the whole "Lord, we just want to thank You for who You are" kind of prayers that we sometimes pray because we want to sound hyperspiritual. But slowly, gradually, I began stripping off the layers of anonymity that shielded my heart from intruders, even my own wife.

Out loud, I told God I was afraid of what I felt was my wife's superior spirituality. I told Him I resented her relationship with Him. I felt she loved Christ more than she loved me. Saying those things aloud then, and even writing them now, seems stupid. But they were real to me, and the results of my saying them were immediate. Deborah and I began connecting at a deep, spiritual level, drawing energy and life from each other like an unbroken circuit.

Deborah always treated my prayer attempts with understanding and was never condescending. I liked hearing the good things she said about me; they made me want to be even better. Meanwhile, she began adjusting her life in such a way that, without compromising her faith and integrity, she could make me feel the importance I wanted to feel in the relationship.

In the end, our prayer together was the key to the success of our marriage. That's where we became intimate—"velcroed at the heart," as we used to joke. Ironically, it was exactly what I wanted from the beginning. I just hadn't known how to get there.

Meanwhile, the deep joy of our physical intimacy was a direct result of the intimacy of our prayer.

During the final twelve years of our marriage, people used to ask me, "What's your secret? What is it that you two have?"

I would reply, only half-joking, "I used to be down on my knees begging for sex. Now I'm down on my knees praying with my wife."

7

Denver

*It got to be the 1960s. All them years I worked for them planta-
tions, the Man didn't tell me there was colored schools I coulda
gone to, or that I coulda learned a trade. He didn't tell me I
coulda joined the army and worked my way up, earned some
money of my own and some respect. I didn't know about World
War II, the war in Korea, or the one in Vietnam. And I didn't
know colored folks had been risin up all around Louisiana for
years, demandin better treatment.*

I didn't know I was different . . .

*I knowed there was other places. I had heard my brother,
Thurman, was out in California stackin hisself some paper
money. So one day, I just decided to head out that way. Didn't
think about it much, just walked out to the railroad tracks and
waited for the train to come a-rollin. There was another fella
hangin around by the tracks, a hobo who'd been ridin the rails*

for a lotta years. He said he'd show me which train was goin to California.

I was about twenty-seven, twenty-eight years old by the time I wound up homeless in Fort Worth. Little children likes to say, "It takes one to know one!" So if you want to know about homeless folks, just ask me 'cause I was one of 'em for a whole lotta years.

Now, there ain't no two ways about it: some homeless folks is just plain ol', no-account lazy. I don't mean to be bad-mouthin nobody, but that's the truth.

On the other hand, though, there's a whole lotta homeless that got that way 'cause they kept tryin and tryin, and no amount a' tryin they done ever amounted to much. You can work a little pickup job for a day and make twenty or thirty dollars. But what you gon' do with twenty or thirty dollars? Maybe you can rent you a room for the night or have a decent meal. But what you gon' do after that?

Did you ever lose somethin or somebody you cared about? Somethin or somebody you really loved? I'm telling you what—if you did, you know that ain't somethin you can get over real easy.

Like I couldn't get rid of the pain when I watched my grandma, Big Mama, get burned to death in her shack. Or when

43

that man ran outta the woods and stabbed my daddy to death. Or when my Aunt Etha, that was takin care a' me after that, took sick and died. All them things happened when I was just a little-bitty boy.

Lotta homeless folks been hurt like that. And the hurt just hangs around you like a stray dog that smells a bone. You can't never get rid of it unless you gets rid of the bone.

I always did believe in Jesus.

Most a' the people on the streets know Jesus loves 'em. But they figure nobody *else* loves 'em *but* Jesus. Street people done heard more sermons than most preachers ever preached. Lotta good folks come 'round the 'hood, talkin 'bout Jesus this, Jesus that. Tellin us about Him is one thing . . . who gon' stick around and *show* us Jesus? See, deliverin kindness ain't the pastor's job. That's our job. When Jesus sent the disciples out two by two, He didn't go with 'em. He stayed back and laid low, maybe had Hisself a cup a' coffee.

Listen at this: Jesus sent the disciples *out*. John and Mark and Nathaniel and them went *into* the villages. When I was homeless, one thing I just couldn't understand is why all these folks kept tryin to invitin me *in* someplace that I didn't wanna be. They'd come out and hand me some kinda piece a' paper, talkin 'bout, "Jesus loves you! Come fellowship with us!" Now, their hearts was in the right place, and they just tryin to show me the love a' God. But seemed like they didn't understand that it just ain't that easy.

For one thing, them folks that invited me was all smilin and clean, and I was all ragged and dirty. 'Sides that, most a' em was white, and I was black as a coffee bean. Wadn't no way I was gon' show up at their church lookin like I looked.

For another thing, where was I gon' leave my bags with all my worldly goods, my blanket and my soap and my half-pint and what have you? It wadn't much, but wadn't no way I was gon' leave it in the 'hood with all them fellas ready to split it up amongst themselves. And I was pretty sure they didn't have no luggage check at the church.

Then they'd say, "God bless you!" and leave me with that piece a' paper so I wouldn't forget where I was s'posed to show up. 'Course, they didn't know I couldn't read.

See, we don't need to be tryin to drag the homeless, or any kinda needy people, to "programs," to "services." What people needs is people.

And needy people don't need no perfect people neither. When Jesus sent His disciples out, He sent Peter right along, knowin Peter had a bad temper and a potty mouth and was gon' deny Him three times. He sent John and James even though they was full a' pride and fightin over the best seat at the table. He even sent Judas, knowin Judas was gon' betray Him. Even though Jesus knowed all a' their sin and weakness, He sent 'em anyway.

Listen, if the devil ain't messin with you, he's already got you. If you is waitin to clean up your own life before you get out and help somebody else, you may as well take off your shoes and crawl back in the bed 'cause it ain't never gon' happen. Jesus don't need no help from no perfect saints. If He did, He wouldn't a' gone up yonder and left us down here in charge.

ASHLEY

Heart Knowledge

By 2004, Matt and Ashley McNeeley's marriage had followed a similar path to mine and Deborah's—troubled and marred with adversity. Matt, then twenty-seven, was an alcoholic who had compromised the marriage. With their daughter only eighteen months old, Ashley, also twenty-seven, was desperate to keep her marriage from crumbling and set a low bar for her expectations. All she wanted was for Matt to be faithful and get sober.

"Once God got me out of the way," Ashley says, "He did so much more."

Matt not only got sober; he also began to lead the Celebrate Recovery program at the McNeeleys' home church, Bent Tree Bible Fellowship in the Dallas suburb of Carrollton, Texas. And the couple's marriage grew strong through their mutual commitment to each other and to their faith.

When Ashley read *Same Kind* at the insistence of her brother-in-law, Josh, she saw in Deborah a kindred spirit, a woman who had decided to ride out marital storms instead of abandoning ship—and who found peaceful waters on the other side. But the book also opened Ashley's eyes to a void in her life.

Her marriage was going well. She was thriving profession-ally. With her sister, Jesse Ihde, she had launched Minerva Consulting, a small but successful marketing and communi-cations consulting firm. But what was she doing to help those who were hungry and homeless and hurting?

"I told my family, we need to get *involved*," she says. "We need to make a difference! We're not doing *anything*."

Through Josh's passion and an uncle who lives in Phoenix, Ashley learned about a program called Open Table. The nonprofit started with a group of men at a Scottsdale, Arizona, church, who worked with youth groups serving at a local homeless shelter. These men realized that their inter-actions at the shelter weren't really helping to break the cycle of homelessness. So they formed the group that would become Open Table, a community of mentors and life coaches who work with individuals and families, creating step-by-step economic stability and wholeness plans to help them get back on their feet.

"The goals are attained through an ongoing management process," the Open Table Web site says, "as well as drawing on resources from the congregation, personal networks, and solutions already created by other Open Table groups." Ashley learned that City of Phoenix officials were backing Open Table and heralding its methods as "best practices" for ending homelessness.

Ongoing management process?

Best practices?

Tackling a social issue through a carefully planned business-model approach seemed to Ashley and Jesse like an ideal fit for them. The sisters decided to launch an Open Table in the Dallas area, and they hit the ground running, creating a business plan, a marketing plan, and a prospectus. They recruited an influential advisor, made the right political connections in the city, and met with Open Table CEO Jon Katov.

Ashley had previous experience with nonprofits, having worked with Verizon on their cause-related marketing programs. She knew people on the boards of several foundations. She was certain she could tap into these connections without the slightest hiccup. "I thought, *I've done this before. Money's just going to fall into our laps, and this isn't going to be any trouble at all.*"

That's not how it went.

At first, every charity Ashley contacted expressed enthusiastic support. But the economic decline of late 2008 was taking its toll on nonprofit organizations, and enthusiasm did not translate into dollars. One by one, each of the board-member relationships Ashley had counted on to help launch Open Table failed to bear fruit. And with no money to pay for marketing and other aspects of their business plan, Ashley and Jesse were forced to shelve the project.

"I was very frustrated that I couldn't get it going," Ashley remembers. At the same time, though, a new realization hit her like cold water in the face. "We were pursuing Open Table with a businesslike model. We had a great handle on all the statistics, the economics of the situation, the demographics. We could really rattle off the numbers about homelessness, but we didn't have heart knowledge about it."

It became evident, Ashley says, that she and Jesse and the people they'd rallied to their cause had spent a lot of time *talking* about doing good in their community, but zero time actually *doing* anything. "We hadn't spent a single minute with people in need. Finally, we thought, *Let's just go* do *it—go serve, and let God work it out.*"

The first stop was the Union Gospel Mission, where Deborah and I first met Denver. Ashley toured the facility with Paul, a volunteer coordinator, and told him that Bent Tree Bible Fellowship would like to get involved.

"Where do you have a need?" Ashley asked.

"Well, we really need someone to hold children's church," Paul told her. He noted that the Union Gospel Mission focused on faith-based recovery and required adult program members to attend chapel. But it was often difficult for home-less parents to get anything out of chapel because they were too distracted managing their children.

"If that's where you have a need, sign us up," Ashley said.

"How many volunteers do you think you can get?" Paul asked.

In that moment, Ashley abandoned her business-plan/

Power Point/action-step instincts and simply jumped. "I have no idea," she said with a grin. "But I can promise you that my husband, brother-in-law, sister, and parents will come."

One Saturday each month, Bent Tree Bible Fellowship began holding children's church for kids aged five to fourteen. The most appealing part, says Ashley, is that the volunteers brought their own children, not to serve but just to participate—singing, doing crafts, and learning Bible stories side by side with homeless kids. "Our hope is that we're making our own kids' worlds just a little bit bigger."

By June 2009, Bent Tree had provided so many volunteers that the Union Gospel Mission was able for the first time to open up a nursery one Saturday each month to care for children under age five. "Volunteers just kept walking in and walking in, until the coordinator said, 'We've never had this many people before!'"

Ashley, planless and happy, just smiled. "Well, here we are!"

When Ashley was conducting her research to start Open Table, she began to understand the *metrics* of homelessness—that, yes, there are X number of homeless people and they're homeless for reasons X, Y, and Z.

"But I didn't recognize that these are people with *stories* and that any of us, all of us, could be there in an instant. The only way to learn that is to go do the work—to meet these people, to know them, to listen to their hearts," Ashley says.

Since getting down to the street level on the issue, there is one point Ashley and Jesse have discussed repeatedly: once you've connected, once you've looked homelessness in the eye, once you know that hundreds of kids in your city go to sleep most nights without a roof over their heads, you have to make a choice either to do something or to consciously turn away.

"You can't forget it, so you have to make a choice," Ashley says. "My sister and I don't think we're doing anything close to important or close to enough. But it's a start."

$\mathcal{8}$

Denver

In 1998, tired of the Park Cities, the Dallas rat race . . . we
returned to Fort Worth. . . . We hadn't been in [town] for
more than a few days when Deborah spied an item in the
Star-Telegram *about homelessness in the city. The piece*
mentioned a place called the Union Gospel Mission. At the
time, an insistent voice in Deborah's heart told her it was a
place she might fit . . .

"I was hoping you'd go with me," she said, smiling and
tilting her head in a way so irresistible I sometimes thought
she should register it for a patent.

The mission, on East Lancaster Street, was tucked deep in
a nasty part of town. While it was true that the murder rate
in Texas had been falling, I was sure that anyone still doing
any murdering probably lived right around there.

I smiled back. "Sure I'll go."

But secretly, I hoped that once she actually rubbed shoulders with the kind of skuzzy derelicts that had robbed my gallery, Deborah would find it too scary, too real, to volunteer on East Lancaster . . .

I should've known better . . .

That night, she dreamed about the mission . . . and this time, about a man.

"It was like that verse in Ecclesiastes," she told me the next morning over breakfast. "A wise man who changes the city. I saw him . . . I saw his face."

I remember when Mr. Ron and Miss Debbie started comin down to the mission. This couple was dressed real nice—not fancy or nothin like that but nice enough to make a lot of us wonder if Mr. Ron was the law.

Funny thing about it was, they started comin one Tuesday and never did stop. Now, we was used to some groups comin ever now and then, or maybe on the holidays, like Thanksgivin or Christmas. Ain't nothin wrong with that, 'cept it makes the homeless feel like they ain't nobody special unless it's some kinda special day.

I can't blame nobody for just comin on the holidays 'cause most folks work, and they can't do nothin but come when it's a vacation day or maybe on the weekends. I can't sling no mud about that 'cause I 'xpect most people doin all they can do. 'Course, if that ain't true, maybe they need to think about that.

Them's the folks I scratch my head about. I just can't figure out why folks go all year without reachin out to help a brother or a sister 'cept on Thanksgivin or Christmas or Easter. It's almost like a light goes on, a lit-up sign in their mind that says, "It's Thanksgivin. I'm gon' serve God," or "It's Christmas. I'm gon' serve God."

What about when it ain't Thanksgivin or Christmas? Is people hungry on other days besides Thanksgivin? Does they need shoes on other days besides Christmas? God treasures the things we do, not because it's a special day or a special time. All things is special when you doin it for God.

But when you reachin out to folks, 'specially if you just reachin out when other folks expects it, you got to ask yourself—is you doin it for God, or is you doin it for you? The things you do for nothin is the things you keep forever. 'Cause when you servin down here 'cause you 'xpect somethin—maybe like your friends is lookin at you like you is some kinda saint, or it's the holidays, and you feel guilty 'cause you ain't done nothin for nobody all year—then you ain't doin it for "nothin." You doin it for somethin. If you doin it for somethin, you already done got paid. God don't pay no overtime.

Don't give yourself credit for what you do. Don't let your right hand know what your left is doin. If you lookin for pride and prestige and glory, you lookin for trouble. We got to put our pride aside and take care a' God's business.

I ain't got no way to read the mind a' God, but I 'xpect part a' His business is makin it Christmas for somebody ever day. If all the Christians—I mean *all* of 'em—got outta the pews on Sundays and into the streets, we'd shut the city down.

We'd shut down hunger.

We'd shut down loneliness.

We'd shut down the notion that there is any such of a thing as a person that don't deserve a kind word and a second chance.

9

Ron

"I'm gon' kill whoever done it!" he screamed. "I'm gon' kill whoever stole my shoes!" Then he sprayed the air with a volley of curses and advanced into the crowd, roundhousing his fists at anyone stupid enough to get in his way . . .

"I think you should try to make friends with him."

"Me!" My eyes widened in disbelief. "Did you not notice that the man you want me to make friends with just threatened to kill twenty people?"

[Deborah] laid her hand on my shoulder and tilted her head with a smile. "I really think God's laid it on my heart that you need to reach out to him."

"Sorry," I said, trying hard to ignore the head tilt, "but I wasn't at that meeting where you heard from God."

After Denver and I struck up our unlikely friendship at the mission, we had a bargain. I was going to show him how to get along with the country-club set, and he was going to show me how to get along in the 'hood. When Deborah first dragged me down to serve at the mission, my biggest worry was catching a disease or some kind of creepy-crawly infestation. But after a while, my heart toward the homeless softened up to the point where I actually started going out into the streets with Denver to reach out to the homeless.

And yet for all of my brand-new do-gooding, I was still a judgmental varmint. I wish I could say that "deep down" I was a judgmental varmint. But no, it was pretty much right there on the surface.

I remember one day in particular when Denver and I went out on the streets surrounding the mission. I had maybe a couple of hundred bucks in cash, and I'd visit with people, ask how they were doing, and bless them with a few dollars.

It's important to draw a distinction between "blessing" the homeless and "helping" the homeless. I used to think I was helping by serving a meal or giving them some clothes, but I found out that for the most part I was just helping myself, making myself feel warm and fuzzy and philanthropic.

To be sure, it is a *blessing* to the homeless when they see people who care. But to really help, you've got to get down in the pit with people and stay with them until they find the strength to get on your shoulders and climb out. Helping someone is when you find out how to help them move toward wholeness and then hang with them until they make a change.

So when Denver and I walked the streets of Fort Worth, it was with the specific intent of bringing blessing. Of stopping to talk to people who are used to folks crossing streets to *avoid* talking to them. Of being a bright smile, a touch of humanity.

It was a crisp, autumn afternoon, and we were heading back toward the mission. I had already made like Santa Claus and passed out almost all the money I had. All I had left was a twenty-dollar bill. Well, we turned a corner and came upon a Hispanic man who looked drunk enough to fry ice cream with his breath. Probably in his fifties, he looked seventy, with gnarled hands and brown skin wrinkled like a crushed grocery sack. Wearing smudged jeans and a threadbare flannel shirt of red lumberjack plaid, he lounged so hard against the brick wall of a streetside warehouse that I couldn't tell whether he was trying to hold himself up or keep the wall from falling down.

Still pretty new to the streets, I pasted on a smile and, with Denver at my shoulder, said to the Hispanic man, "What can I do for you today?"

As the man tried to focus his eyes on me, a thin strand of drool slid from the corner of his mouth and began traveling south. "I needsh a reedle moony," he slurred in a heavy Spanish accent.

I didn't quite catch what he said and asked him to repeat himself.

"He say he needs a little money," Denver said over my shoulder.

I am not giving a drunk a twenty-dollar bill, I thought as I watched the drool reach the Hispanic man's chin. Smiling away, I dug into my pants pockets, feeling for smaller change.

Finding none, I pulled out the twenty-dollar bill and surreptitiously showed it to Denver. Glancing back at my mentor in the 'hood, I tried intently to telegraph a message with my eyes: *If I give him my last twenty, all he's going to do is go down to the liquor store and buy some more booze!*

Suddenly Denver leaned in, and I felt his breath at my ear. "Don't judge the man," he said, low and quiet. "Just give him the twenty dollars."

Reluctantly, I held out the money, and the man took it. Just at that moment, the southbound drop of drool detached itself from his chin and hurtled toward the sidewalk.

"Shank ew," he said.

I had never stopped smiling, but now my grin felt as fake as a plugged nickel. I felt like I'd just given a push to a suicide jumper.

Denver and I bid the man good-bye and headed down the street toward the mission. We hadn't gone thirty yards when Denver stopped. "Turn 'round here and look at me, Mr. Ron. I wanna tell you somethin."

I stopped and faced Denver, and in a way that was becoming familiar to me, he pinned me with one eye while squinting the other like Clint Eastwood. "That man you just gave that money to—his name is José. And he ain't drunk. He's a stroke victim. And he's one a' the hardest workin men I ever knowed."

Denver went on to tell me that before a stroke got him, José had been a bricklayer and a rock mason who worked hard, lived cheap, and sent all his money home to Mexico to support his family.

"He don't even drink, Mr. Ron," Denver said. "He depends on people like you to eat."

Immediately, I thought of Deborah. From the moment we set foot in the mission, she had looked beyond the ragged clothes and the scars and the dirt and the smells. It was as though God had given her X-ray vision to see right past all that to the people underneath.

She never asked them, "How did you get in the shape you're in?" Her thinking was, if you condition your offer of help on how a needy person got that way, you're probably not going to help very many people. The question Deborah asked was, "What is your need *now*?"

Now Denver completed his verdict and gave me an ultimatum. Keeping me pinned with that eyeball, he said, "You know what you did? You judged a man without knowin his heart. And I'm gon' tell you somethin. If you gon' walk these streets with me, you gon' have to learn how to serve these people without judgin 'em. Let the judgin be up to God."

Denver's pronouncements on judgment reminded me of a

letter that the painter Vincent Van Gogh once wrote to his brother, Theo. The subject was idleness and whether anyone can truly look at a man who appears to be lazy—or drunk or otherwise indigent—and make an accurate judgment:

Sometimes . . . [a person's] right to exist has a justification that is not always immediately obvious to you . . . Someone who has been wandering about for a long time, tossed to and fro on a stormy sea, will in the end reach his destination. Someone who has seemed to be good for nothing, unable to fill any job, any appointment, will find one in the end and, energetic and capable, will prove himself quite different from what he seemed at first . . .

I should be very happy if you could see in me something more than a kind of . . . [an idler]. For there is a great difference between one idler and another idler. There is someone who is an idler out of laziness and lack of character, owing to the baseness of his nature. If you like, you may take me for one of those. Then there is the other kind of idler, the idler despite himself, who is inwardly consumed by a great longing for action who does nothing because his hands are tied, because he is, so to speak, imprisoned somewhere, because he lacks what he needs to be productive, because disastrous circumstances have brought him forcibly to this end. Such a one does not always know what he can do, but he nevertheless instinctively feels, I am good for something! My existence is not without reason! I know that I could be a quite a different person! How can I be of use, how can I be of service? There is something inside me, but what can it be? He is quite another idler. If you like you may take me for one of those.

A caged bird in spring knows perfectly well that there is some way in which he should be able to serve. He is well aware that there is something to be done, but he is unable to do it . . . "What a idler," says another bird passing by—what an idler . . . But then the season of the great migration arrives, an attack of melancholy. He has everything he needs, say the children who tend him in his cage—but he looks out, at the heavy thundery sky, and in his heart of hearts he rebels against his fate. I am caged, I am caged and you say I need nothing, you idiots! I have everything I need, indeed! Oh! please give me the freedom to be a bird like other birds!

A kind of idler of a person resembles that kind of idler of a bird. And people are often unable to do anything, imprisoned as they are in I don't know what kind of terrible, terrible, oh such terrible cage . . .

A justly or unjustly ruined reputation, poverty, disastrous circumstances, misfortune, they all turn you into a prisoner. You cannot always tell what keeps you confined, what immures you, what seems to bury you, and yet you can feel those elusive bars, railings, walls . . .

Do you know what makes the prison disappear? Every

deep, genuine affection. Being friends, being brothers, loving, that is what opens the prison, with supreme power, by some magic force. Without these one stays dead. But whenever affection is revived, there life revives. Moreover, the prison is sometimes called prejudice, misunderstanding, fatal ignorance of one thing or another, suspicion . . .

If you could see me as something other than a idler of the bad sort, I should be very happy.

DARLENE

Skid Row Samaritan

During the Gold Rush, Sacramento, California, was a thriving place, the westernmost stop for stagecoaches and wagon trains, for the first transcontinental railroad and even the Pony Express. Sacramento still thrives today, but like many cities, it has also become the last stop in life for thousands of homeless people.

Homelessness is not new to the city, but in early 2009 it was getting worse. National attention focused on a tent city that had sprung up on the city's outskirts. As many as fifty new people a week moved in, some of them as a result of the avalanche of home foreclosures, a phenomenon that hit Sacramento harder than most US cities.

But the tent city was not the only part of Sacramento where homelessness was a problem. The wedge of town west of the capitol was a motley mix of redevelopment and still-derelict, a place where attempts at gentrification competed with rundown motels that doubled as low-income housing for transients. The city was working to fix up the area, but for longtime Sacramento residents, those streets still meant drugs, prostitution, and shabby bands of the hardcore homeless. It

was a part of the city, Darlene Garcia told us, that she pre-
ferred to avoid.

But Darlene, age sixty-six, did find herself driving through
west Sacramento on her way home from on errand on a cold,
cloudy day early in 2009. And sure enough, as she drove
along a seedy thoroughfare near the Pickwood Hotel, she saw
a man sprawled on the ground in a narrow vacant lot between
buildings.

"He was lying on the ground close to the sidewalk,"
Darlene remembers. "If he had been under the tree that was
nearby, I would have thought he was lying there sleeping
because that's what people do in that area."

As it was, Darlene's first thought was that the man was
probably a drunk who had passed out in public. But something about the way he was lying there stirred her concern.
Then Denver Moore flashed into her mind, and something
about his story, which she had just read, helped her think
twice about snap judgments.

Darlene slowed her car. "There was a lot of traffic,
people driving right past this man, walking past him on the
sidewalk."

Forced to keep driving because of the flow of traffic,
Darlene sped up again. But the farther she advanced down
the block, the more she knew she had to go back.

Darlene circled the block and returned to the spot near

the Pickwood. The man hadn't moved. She parked along the curb, cars whizzing past, and got out, intensely aware of being a lone woman on foot in a "bad" part of town.

She walked to the man and stood over him. He appeared to be sleeping. His clothes were older but not ragged. He appeared younger than Darlene, but his face was haggard and pale.

"Are you all right?" she asked.

The man opened his eyes very slightly and whispered, "I'm having a heart attack."

Darlene's pulse quickened. "How do you know?"

He raised his hand to his chest. "Because it . . . hurts . . . right . . . here."

Darlene snatched her cell phone from her purse and quickly punched in 911. Then she ran to the curb, waving her arms, trying to flag down help. An older gentleman stopped and joined Darlene; his presence made her feel a little safer. The two waited a few more minutes as emergency crews rolled up to the scene and began treating the man.

When she saw he was in good hands, Darlene got in her car and drove home. On the way, she reflected on the step she'd just taken. She had helped people all her life, spending decades teaching preschool in a state program for low-income families and even buying shoes, clothes, and food for some families who had none. But before she read about Denver, she says, "I would never have had the nerve to go back. I wouldn't have felt safe stopping in that area. But this time I wasn't scared. I thought, *I have to do this.*"

Darlene went home and telephoned her best friend to share what had happened. "I think I might have saved someone's life today," she said.

"That's good," her friend replied. "But you have to be careful in that neighborhood."

"I know," said Darlene and smiled.

10

Denver

*Don't get me wrong. Wadn't like I was clean and sober all the
time, neither. Just 'cause me and Mr. Ron was friends don't
mean I turned into no overnight saint. We might a' been goin
out to fancy places in the daytime. But at night I'd still go out
to the hobo jungle and pass around the Jim Beam with the
fellas.*

Now, I ain't sayin that ever time you see a drunk you got to
give him a dollar. I'm just sayin everbody you give a dollar
to ain't necessarily a drunk. I remember that time Mr. Ron didn't
wanna give José that twenty-dollar bill, and I told him to quit
worryin about what the man was gon' do with the money and
just be a blessin to him.

I know a lotta people worry 'bout the same thing. If I give

that homeless man some money, what he gon' do with it? Buy hisself a half-pint or a beer?

Since my book came out, I been to a lotta parties and sophisticated places, and everbody in there be talkin 'bout, "Gimme a glass a' red wine."

Now, how come ain't nobody sayin somethin 'bout them havin wine, but they got a problem with a homeless man havin wine? Ain't you ever seen a rich alcoholic? And who you think needs the wine worse? You think anybody *wants* to be a drunk? You kiddin me, right? They ain't havin no fun.

Now you might say, "The homeless man ain't got enough money to be spendin none on wine. That's irresponsible. If you give money to a homeless man, he needs to be spendin it on food."

Maybe you right. The thing about it is, though, gifts is free. When you give a person a gift, you is also givin that person the freedom to do whatever they want with it. When you give a homeless man a dollar, you ain't sayin, "Here. Go buy yourself a chicken." If you really wanted him to have some food, you'd take him in the McDonald's and buy him a Big Mac and a apple pie.

No, when you give a homeless man a dollar, what you really sayin is, "I see you. You ain't invisible. You is a person." I tells folks to look at what's written on all that money they be givin away: it says "In God We Trust." You just be the blessin. Let God worry about the rest.

Sometime, when you reach out to a homeless person, might

seem like to you she's throwed off in her mind. Like she ain't got no sense. But sometimes things ain't exactly the way they look. Like a friend a' mine asked me one time, said she seen a homeless lady standin at a intersection. This lady was real skinny and her clothes was dirty and they didn't match. She didn't have no sign that said, "Will work 4 food" or "God bless!" She was lookin up at the sky, swayin back and forth, and talkin to the clouds in a voice like a little girl.

My friend said she felt bad 'cause she was scared to give the lady any money, scared she had somethin wrong with her.

"Wadn't nothin wrong with her," I told my friend. "Sound like to me she just didn't want to be bothered."

But a lotta times there *is* somethin wrong with homeless folks. Mr. Don Shisler down at the Union Gospel Mission told me one time he thinks about six or seven outta ever ten homeless has got some kinda mental problem. At one point, they was regular folks like you that might sit around and read a book 'bout folks like them. But somethin happened to em that got em throwed off.

Maybe a fella's wife throwed him out, so he went to live with his cousin. Then his cousin throwed him out, so he wound up on the street. I ain't sayin he didn't do nothin to deserve it. Maybe he did, but that don't mean he ain't still one a' God's children.

I remember when I rolled into Fort Worth on that freight train. It wadn't too long after that president named Kennedy got shot dead in Dallas. I used to camp out in the hobo jungle at night and panhandle for food during the daytime.

71

Some homeless fellas taught me a trick called "the hamburger drop." That's when you get you a little money, say about a dollar, and you go down to the McDonald's or the Burger King and buy yourself a cheap burger. Then you go to some fancy part a' town where everybody got on coats and ties and workin in them big glass buildins. Now, this don't work unless you can find a buildin with a trash can out front. Once you spot it, you take a coupla bites out that burger, then—when you sure nobody's comin— you stash that burger down in that trash can real careful.

Now you wait till you see somebody comin, and when you do, you act like you diggin in the garbage for food, and then you pop up with that burger and start eatin it.

Nine times outta ten, them rich folks is gon' stop you cold and yell, "Hey, don't eat that!" Then they gon' give you some money and tell you to go buy yourself somethin to eat.

When I first got to Fort Worth, I remember a lotta times wishin that instead of givin me money, somebody'd just ask me my name. But after a while, when I figured out city folks thought I wadn't no better than a speck a' dust, my heart began to grow a tough hide over it, like a orange that's been left out in the sun. My heart got harder and harder. Pretty soon, all I wanted was for folks to gimme that dollar and leave me alone.

That's when homeless folks that ain't drinkin or druggin already make themselves a new friend. Them half-pints and beers and little packets a' white powder becomes their friend, their pastor, their storm shelter—a deep, dark, hummin hole they can

72

crawl into to escape from themselves even if it's just for a little while. They tryin to drown their problem—or burn it.

Now whatever drove them to the streets from the get-go is a problem, and whatever they is usin to escape is a problem.

So now they got two problems.

11

Ron

That Deborah would get cancer made no more sense than a drive-by shooting. She was the most health-conscious person I had ever known. She didn't eat junk food or smoke. She stayed fit and took vitamins. There was no history of cancer in her family. Zero risk factors.

What Denver had said three weeks earlier haunted me: Those precious to God become important to Satan. Watch your back, Mr. Ron! Somethin bad fixin to happen to Miss Debbie.

Just before midnight she stirred. I stood and leaned over her bed, my face pressed close to hers. Her eyes opened, drowsy with narcotics. "Is it in my liver?"

"Yes." I paused and looked down at her, trying vainly to drive sadness from my face. "But there's still hope."

She closed her eyes again, and the moment I had dreaded for hours passed quickly without a single tear. My own dry eyes didn't surprise me—I had never really learned how to cry. But now life had presented a reason to learn, and I yearned for a river of tears, a biblical flood. Maybe my broken heart would teach my eyes what to do.

At age seventy-five, my daddy was diagnosed with prostate cancer. Even though the doctors said it was slow-growing and that he would probably die of something else, he called us all together to say good-byes and give him last rites, even though he wasn't Catholic. I guess he reasoned he was entitled since he'd voted for Kennedy. My brother led him in the sinner's prayer. Daddy repeated it after John and said he understood that he was praying Christ would forgive him of his sins.

I was skeptical. And it made Daddy mad when I reminded him that his doctors weren't at all worried that he was at death's door. No doubt he was feeling his mortality and begging for the attention that I had spent a lifetime withholding.

Four years later, in April 1999, Deborah was diagnosed with a very aggressive form of colon and liver cancer. Some doctors thought she might only live three months; others thought a year. Though her prognosis was catastrophic, we were not going down without a fight, and she began a very aggressive chemotherapy regimen, sometimes alternating different treatments within the same week. The drugs took her down swiftly, but she fought like the last warrior left standing at Troy. Deborah had a lot to live for, like seeing her dream of revival coming to our city through

Denver. She also longed to see Regan and Carson get married and to be a grandmother to the grandchildren she had prayed for since our children became our own.

On Christmas Day of that year, Deborah did something heroic. She cooked a gourmet dinner at Rocky Top, the 350-acre ranch we had bought in 1990, and she decorated it in the style of the authentic Old West. Don't ask how she did it. No one can explain that. But with her elegance and style, all Deborah's special dinners were fit for royalty, and they usually included an invitation to Denver and to the ungrateful "Earl of Haltom," a noble title I had bestowed on my dad as a joke. (We had moved to the Fort Worth suburb of Haltom City when I was seven.)

As we took our places at the table, we blessed the food and praised God for the strength he had given Deborah to prepare it. And, of course, we asked for healings. I'm sure he meant no malice, but before the first bite, Dad commented, "Cancer ain't no big deal. I've had prostate cancer for four years, and it don't bother me a bit. Y'all are making a big deal about nothin!"

Deborah left the table in tears. Daddy was angry that she left the table. He looked at my mother and said, "Let's go home Tommye. We're not welcome here!"

They left. Denver walked them to their car. The meal went into the refrigerator. Carson, Regan, and I crawled into bed with Deborah.

Denver acted as though he was very uncomfortable but

avoided taking sides. It was his second Christmas with us, and he was confused. He took a walk down by the river to gather his thoughts, then returned to the house and knocked on our door.

"Bless him," he told me when I answered it.

"Who?"

"Your daddy. He meant no wrong, and I praise God for your father and his life. He's a good man, and he's a part of my blessin. If it hadn't been for your father, there wouldn't be no Mr. Ron. And if it hadn't been for you and Miss Debbie, I'd still be in the bushes instead of havin Christmas with you.

"I want you to hear me real good on this, Mr. Ron. Just bless him."

I listened to what Denver had to say and acted as though I planned to take his advice. But the truth was, I thought his advice was ill informed at best and possibly tainted by the fact that he was used to living around all manner of addicts and alcoholics. Besides, Denver had no idea of the hell and embarrassment Earl Hall had put my family through over the years. And even if Denver had a small point—that there was more to the man than the "Earl in the bottle"—I wasn't ready to let him out.

12

Ron

I was fifty-five, graying at the temples, with half my heart lying in the ground at Rocky Top. How to survive? How to move forward? I felt trapped in a whiteout snowstorm with no guide and fresh out of supplies. The intensity of my fear surprised me.

For weeks, I wandered through the house like a ghost in a graveyard. I haunted Deborah's closet, opening the drawers and cabinets, touching her scarves, her stockings, burying my face in her clothes, trying to breathe in her scent. Sometimes I closed the closet door behind me and sat there in the dark, holding the last photograph ever taken of us together.

On November 3, 2000, my wife of thirty-one years and seven days passed into eternity. Cancer took her, but I blamed God more than cancer for ripping her away from me and shredding my heart in the process.

For a couple of weeks, a whirl of activity blunted my new reality—the private graveside service where we buried Deborah in her favorite spot at Rocky Top, the church memorial service, a getaway with my son and daughter meant to help us process our grief. But then the busyness was done, and I stood at the edge of the yawning black chasm that was a life without my wife.

I paced the halls, crying, tears running down my face in sheets. I couldn't stop. And nothing that anyone could say seemed to help.

Worst of all were the expressions of Christian sympathy.

"You know, Ron, we've been praying for Deborah to be healed," some well-meaning person would say. "And now she's healed forever."

Bull, I thought. *She's dead.*

In my blackest moments, I might even have said that out loud. It angered me that people might think some pat little Christian phrase would quench the inferno of my grief. At other times, I realized people meant well and, mainly, spoke wounding words because they didn't know what else to say.

There were just a couple of people who did know what to say: "I can't even imagine how you must be feeling, but I just want you to know that I love you." Those were the people who climbed down with me into the pit of my grief and stayed with me. But the grief pit is a pretty nasty, slimy place, and most people don't want to get down in it.

To keep them from having to, I withdrew from everyone, even

my friends. I just wanted to disappear. And at times, it seemed I *was* disappearing—literally. Inside of three weeks, I lost twenty-five pounds. The bones of my face cut sharp angles. My clothes flapped on my frame, an empty husk where a man used to be.

I didn't want anyone to see me, even if I had a decent day. I felt that if I looked happy, someone would mistake that for meaning I was doing well. I did not want to do well. I wanted my time in sackcloth and ashes and did not want to be robbed of it. I would go to the grocery store at two in the morning just so I wouldn't have to see anyone.

Psychologists like to talk about the stages of grief: anger, bargaining, denial, depression, acceptance. For a long time after Deborah died, I stayed stuck in anger like a tractor stuck in the mud on a Texas blackland farm after a pouring rain. To call it *anger* seems too mild. You can be angry over a broken dish or a lost football game. This was profound rage, and it had one primary target:

> *As I fired arrows of blame—at the doctors, the pharmaceutical industry, cancer researchers—clearly the bull's-eye was God. It was He who had ripped a gaping and irreparable hole in my heart. Without a gun or mask, He robbed me of my wife and stole my children's mother and my grandchildren's grandmother. I had trusted Him, and He had failed me.*

I was afraid to be real about that. I knew most of my Christian friends would not understand my anger. They all wanted me to take a different path than I took, to praise God for His divine plan, to resign myself to His will.

Instead, I sat in my room alone, screaming at Him, "If that's what You do to the people who love You most, I don't want to love You!"

Sometimes I wished one of my Christian friends would just be real with me. That one of them would say something like, "Can you believe what God did? It doesn't seem fair!"

It might have comforted me if they'd said that. Since Deborah's death, I try never to mute another person's grief with some kind of verbal anesthetic. Instead, I try to just cry with them and sometimes even to simply say, "Yeah, that stinks."

But even as I wished someone would be that real with me in my grief, a truth nagged at the back of my mind. It percolated way down in the blue pool of my soul, where there lay a small inlet somehow unfouled by rage: God did the same thing to His own son—ordained for him an excruciatingly painful death.

And Jesus said, "No servant is better than his Master."

If anyone I had ever known was a servant of God, it was my wife. She did not want to die, but she did want to serve God. And she had, serving Him—through serving the homeless—right up until the moment when her body would no longer allow it.

Shortly after Deborah died, her best friend, Mary Ellen, shared with me that verse from the gospel of John that I mentioned earlier: "Truly, truly, I say to you, unless a grain of wheat falls into the earth and dies, it remains alone; but if it dies, it bears much fruit."

Within weeks of Deborah's death, more than half a million dollars had poured into the Union Gospel Mission—money designated to build a chapel and state-of-the-art facility that would help homeless men, women, and children in Deborah's name. By 2009, Deborah's story had raised more than thirty million dollars for homeless shelters around America.

Do I wish God could've managed to help the homeless without taking my wife?

Absolutely.

Do I believe Deborah, if she could now see the fruit, would want to come back?

Absolutely not.

The pain of losing her still brings tears, especially when I play with my three granddaughters—granddaughters Deborah never got to meet. But Denver met them for her. Griffin, my daughter Regan's girl, is now three and a half. When she was born in 2005, she was the first white baby Denver ever held.

———

Daddy cried at Deborah's funeral, said she always treated him with respect. A year later, we broke ground for the new homeless mission and chapel to be named after her down on East Lancaster. Mama came, as well as the mayor and several state legislators.

Dad stayed home.

"What's all the big deal raising money and building buildings for the homeless?" he groused. "They ain't nothin but a bunch of drunks and addicts. They got themselves in the mess. Let 'em get out on their own."

He endeared himself to me further with this addition: "If you wanna give a bunch of money to someone, why don't you give it to me?"

"What would you spend it on?" I asked.

"I'd buy better whiskey—Jack Daniels instead of Jim Beam!"

It irritated Dad to no end that I spent far more time with Denver than with him. And even worse, every time I visited him, Denver was with me. Earl Hall had definitely been a racist. He claimed to have taken a cure and gotten over it, but I didn't believe him.

Dad told me it wasn't right for a man to live alone and that a very beautiful person was going to move in with me—*him*. I actually thought that was funny, and for the first time I caught a glimpse of his humor with fresh vision. But a couple of months later, it dang near killed him when I moved Denver in with me instead of him.

Lupe Murchison, John D.'s fabulously wealthy widow, had followed her husband into glory, leaving two hundred million dollars to charity. The Murchison family asked me to move into the estate and sell off the Murchison art collection, which was valued at around ten million dollars. I invited Denver to move in with me and help me guard the place. That meant Daddy had to stay in Haltom City. When it came to sowing and reaping, I tallied that as a fair deal.

CARINA

Rearview Mirror

As the mother of four boys, from toddler to age eight, Carina Delacanal had very little time to herself. In 2007, she learned she might not have much time left at all.

Carina, then twenty-nine, had just given birth to her youngest son, Joshua. And while three boys plus a new baby could drive any woman to distraction, Carina began to think that something might actually be wrong with her. "I noticed I was more forgetful than usual," Carina remembers. "Just for peace of mind, I went to see my doctor."

Peace was not what she found.

"The news isn't as good as I'd hoped," the doctor told Carina when the results of a CAT scan came back. "You have what we call an arteriovenous malformation (AVM) on the right side of your brain."

An AVM is something like an aneurysm, the doctor explained, a weakness in the wall of a blood vessel. Carina had been born with hers, and if it ruptured, she could die instantly. Her only option: brain surgery, either conventional or with a radiological gamma knife.

"I felt so overwhelmed," Carina says. "I wanted to hear

God's audible voice tell me where to go, who to see, what procedure to choose."

But questions tore at her heart:

"Why? Why me? Why this, why now? My children need their mommy! Why would God tear me away from them?"

Before the diagnosis, Carina had been a harried mom who barely had time for her daily devotional reading. Now she dove into the Scriptures, clinging to those that quickened her heart and writing them down in a notebook.

She sought counsel from her pastor and proceeded "cautiously, in baby steps," asking God and each doctor for wisdom. All the while, Carina poured out her anguish and concern in her notebook.

"Why?" she still wanted know. "What possible purpose could this serve?"

The risk of death loomed like a phantom. But there was another risk: even if doctors could repair the AVM, they said, the surgery could leave the left side of Carina's body paralyzed for life.

After weeks of painstaking research, Carina selected Don Woodson, a renowned Phoenix neurosurgeon, to perform her operation. And she continued to battle her fear with prayer. "I asked that the Lord's hands be on the surgeon's hands as he operated on me."

When the time for the procedure neared, Carina flew to

Arizona and checked into the ICU of the hospital where the surgery would be performed. The day before the procedure, a nurse came to check on her. Still gripped with anxiety and looking for comfort, Carina asked her, "What kind of surgeon is Dr. Woodson? What's his reputation here?"

The nurse offered a reassuring smile. "When Dr. Woodson is in surgery, it's as if God is using his hands."

Carina's heart soared! It was as if the nurse had spoken aloud the answer to her prayer.

The next day, Carina emerged from surgery with full mobility and her AVM successfully repaired. Back at home, members of her church beat a steady path to the Delacanals' home, bearing meals and offering babysitting. One close friend also brought a stack of books.

"As a mother of four boys, I have very little time for myself, so just reading my devotion for the day was a huge accomplishment for me," Carina says. "I was about to give the books back when my friend pulled one from the stack and held it out."

"This book was very special to me," she said.

Carina glanced at the title: *Same Kind of Different as Me*. She was unimpressed. Still, to be gracious, she thanked her friend and took the book. That day, with little to do but sit still and let her brain heal, she lay in bed and turned to page 1. And before too many pages had gone by, she says, "It was as if God gave me new eyes to see and new ears to hear!"

Reading the story of Denver's slavelike upbringing and his eighteen years spent homeless on the streets of Fort Worth, of Deborah's cancer diagnosis and her battle against all odds, and of our crazily unlikely friendship gave Carina a new perspective on the terrible trial she'd just been through.

"I began to laugh to myself, wondering if I went through all that I did just to get me to sit down and read this amazing true testimony," she told us. "It went to my hands, through my eyes, and straight to my heart!"

With her new eyes, Carina could see with crystalline clarity God's shepherding kindness in her own life. The trial by fire of illness had drawn her and her husband closer, like two lovers huddled together before a campfire on a bitterly cold night. In fact, their season of fear had drawn her whole family closer to each other and closer to God.

In addition, knowing she could have lost forever the ability to use the left side of her body gave her new appreciation for what she was able to do. "I would never again take for granted the gift of serving," she says. Now the simple ability to change her baby's diaper by herself seemed a miracle.

That she had children at all was a miracle too. During consultations leading up to her surgery, doctors had told her that if they'd found the AVM before she had children, they would have advised her to avoid getting pregnant at all costs. Each of her pregnancies could easily have caused the AVM to burst.

But that hadn't happened. Suddenly Carina could see that God had protected her every day of her life, only revealing the AVM *after* she had four beautiful, healthy sons.

"Our pastor had an explanation for why I didn't realize until later how God had held my hand every step of the way," Carina says. "He says sometimes you can only understand *why* things happen when you see them in the rearview mirror."

13

Ron

Like country folks, we sat around Deborah's grave on hay bales . . . For the next hour and a half, we honored my wife. We sang old-time spirituals and country hymns, accompanied by two cowboy friends playing acoustic guitars. Warm sunlight filtered through the oaks, casting circles of gold on Deborah's pine casket, so that the simple box she'd asked for appeared covered in shimmering medallions.

Two weeks after we buried Deborah, Denver and I drove back to Rocky Top. We'd buried her in a simple casket, covering the grave with a pile of rocks and marking the spot with a cross of cedar. The ranch is crawling with critters, from bobcats to wild hogs. Worried that wild animals might try to dig her up, I hadn't slept since. Denver and I were on our way back to build a fence of stones and wrought iron around the grave.

For more than an hour, we rolled west from Dallas in complete silence. Then, just as we crossed the railroad tracks in the little town of Brazos, Denver burst into laughter, as though bumping over the rails had shaken loose some buried joy. I shot him a sideways glare, irritated that he would find something to laugh about when God had seen fit to steal my wife.

"What is so dang funny?" I asked.

"Mr. Ron, there ain't nobody gon' believe our story," he spit out between chuckles. "We got to write us a book."

"Who is this 'we,' Kemo Sabe? You can't read or write . . . just who is going to write it?"

"Well, I'll tell you my part, and you write it down. You know your part, so you write that down. Then we'll put it together and make us a book."

Three weeks later, we raised the gates at what had gone from a lonesome stone-covered grave to a little family cemetery we named Brazos de Dios, which means "the arms of God." There was so far only one family member in residence, but I knew I would join Deborah there someday, near her favorite spot where a leaning oak sheltered a natural stone bench in a covering of shade. Meanwhile, though, I had a problem. Half my heart was buried in the ground at Rocky Top. What exactly did God expect me to do now? Could He possibly want me to write a book with Denver? And if He did, what would I write?

I thought I'd begin my search for answers in Europe. During my art-dealing career, I had often found Italy a refuge. I loved the pace of life there—walking up narrow stone streets, waiting for the pizza place to open, finding a vista and a sidewalk café where the only thing you have to do is dip your biscotti in your espresso. I'd spent wonderful times in the village of Positano, famous for lemons so bountiful that the scent of them floats on the air all summer. And who could resist the food—*bombulonis* (fresh-fried donuts), fresh gelato with crushed raspberries, that wonderful pizza. People might think I'd be looking at art, but when I'm in Italy, I'm eating.

And now maybe, I'd be eating . . . and writing.

After a ten-hour flight, I landed in Rome and checked in at the Hotel Columbus, located a stone's throw from the Holy See. Standing in the cavernous lobby, I gazed up at the frescoed ceilings arching overhead, marked with beams of dark wood painted with geometric designs. The lobby had been slightly modernized, but through a broad passage I could see the colonnade leading back to the pope's former residence, which stood right at the very entrance to the Vatican.

A coincidence struck me. The Hotel Columbus was named for an explorer who five hundred years before had set out on an adventure. With little to go on but faith, he'd braved treacherous seas to discover a new land. Now here I was, fifty-five years old and also facing a new land, a new future entirely different from the one I'd envisioned less than two years before. But unlike Columbus, who was commissioned by a king to discover a new world, my King had exiled me to a world I hated bitterly, a world without my wife. And unlike Columbus, I had no faith. Mine lay six feet down at Rocky Top, having been buried deeper with every turn of the grave diggers' spades.

As I went through the motions of checking in, I reflected that I didn't really have a solid plan for how I would begin to write Deborah's story down. I only had some fuzzy notion of camping out in this venerable building and scribbling down the memories now darting around in my mind like ghosts. I was sure many prayers had been lifted to heaven from the old rooms over my head. The pope had lived in this building, after all, so I figured God had to be familiar with the address. Maybe He would see me here, clinging to my pen, and help usher my task along.

It was not to be. I had barely settled into my room, with a view of Via della Conciliazione, the grand boulevard leading into the Vatican, when a fresh storm of grief blew through my heart like a typhoon. Day after day, I sat by the weathered windows, staring out at the Holy See. My anguish was a black chasm, the pain physical, as though grief were a fanged monster that had invaded my torso and was feeding on me from the inside out. I felt condemned and abandoned, self-righteous in my anger with God.

In certain moments, I was struck by a realization that I had it better than most, and I felt a little guilty for grieving so extravagantly. After all, who would commiserate with a poor millionaire relegated to a fifteenth-century palace to sip Pinot Grigio while nursing his broken heart? Suddenly, I grieved for the thousands of people who buried their spouses on Sunday and had to show back up at work on Monday to earn money to pay for the funeral. By comparison, I had been blessed. For the two years of Deborah's cancer battle, I had been able to set aside my work and stay at her side. Now I could afford to take some time to heal. This thought, at least, was a lighted buoy that flashed a glimmer of gratitude over the dark sea of my rage.

But it wasn't enough to move me past despair. Not yet. Rome's aura of romance, art, and architecture had rolled up like a cheap window shade, replaced by images of Nero at the Coliseum and me being dragged off and fed to the lions. Unable to write, I decamped and took a train to Florence, managing not to blame my lack of literary productivity on the pope.

I arrived on a cold, snowy day, unusual for Florence, and moved into Villa Angeli—Villa of Angels—a fifteenth-century country retreat tucked into the hills above Florence, just below a monastery in the tiny Etruscan village of Fiesole. Built seventy years before Columbus discovered America, the property was known as one of the most beautiful villas in the world. My friends Julio and Pilar Larraz, who live there, offered me refuge. My bedroom offered a view of the red-tile roofs of Tuscany below and, above, the monastery nestled in an ancient olive grove.

There in the Villa of Angels, I finally began writing. Scribbling in blue ink on a yellow legal pad, I poured out scenes of hope and trepidation: the first day Deborah and I went to the mission. Hope and fear: the first day we met Denver. Hope and victory: the formation of deep friendships with Denver and other homeless. Hope and terror: Deborah's cancer diagnosis and her nineteen-month battle to live. Then hope extinguished, replaced by desolation: where I had lived since she died.

As I wrote, I paused for long moments and gazed across the misty Tuscan hills at the Duomo, Florence's central cathedral, consecrated in 1436. No one could deny that I had landed in one of the most beautiful spots in the world, a backdrop of living inspiration for great artists and writers from Dante to da Vinci to Michelangelo. But for me the city that so inspired them was cloaked in the colors of mourning—smoggy grays and charcoal black, shroud colors unsuitable for the joyful journey that was Deborah's life.

I reread what I had written so far and thought of the first important exhibition of modern art in America, the New York Armory Show of 1913, where critics lacerated the works on display, declaring they weren't even worthy to be tossed in an ash can.

Those works of art didn't merit that criticism, but my first written words did. Before returning to Texas, I tossed them in the trash.

I don't know if it happened on the train ride to Rome or while clearing customs at the airport. But somewhere inside me, a switch flipped. And on the eleven-hour flight home, the words began to flow in earnest, faster than my hand could drive my Hotel Columbus ballpoint pen.

Although I know they were there, the people sharing my row of airline seats vanished. I don't recall eating the cardboard-flavored in-flight chicken that I'm certain I was offered. I only remember being shocked, as the first officer announced our final approach to Dallas, to find I'd written ninety longhand pages—a manuscript longer than any term paper I had ever written at Texas Christian University and all without Cliff's Notes.

Bleary-eyed, I trudged through US customs, clutching my newborn manuscript. At the baggage claim, I looked up to find three grinning ladies clustered around me.

"Excuse me. We don't mean to bother you," said the one sporting a Gucci bag and a lilting Texas accent. "We couldn't help but notice that you wrote and wrote all the way from Rome, and you look real familiar. Are you by chance a famous writer?"

I smiled, exhausted. "No, I'm not famous, and I'm not a writer. But I am working on a book."

"What kind of book?" the lady asked, glancing excitedly at her companions.

I thought for a second. How could I summarize the maelstrom of compassion, pain, friendship, redemption, and grief that had been my life for the past four years?

Finally, an answer hit me.

"A love story," I said.

14

Denver

"I want you to know that I forgive you," Deborah said [to the woman I had had an affair with]. "I hope you find someone who will not only truly love you but honor you."

Her grace stunned me. But not nearly so much as what she said next: "I intend to work on being the best wife Ron could ever want, and if I do my job right, you will not be hearing from my husband again."

Deborah quietly placed the phone in its cradle, sighed with relief, and locked her eyes on mine. "You and I are now going to rewrite the future history of our marriage."

She wanted to spend a couple of months in counseling, she said, so we could figure out what was broken, how it got that way, and how to fix it. "If you'll do that," she said, "I'll forgive you. And I promise I will never bring this up, ever again."

for the next three and a half years, mostly at Lupe Murchison's breakfast table, me and Mr. Ron wrote us a book. Of course, I couldn't write or read at the time, but I told Mr. Ron everthing I could remember, and he wrote it all down.

But we hadn't been workin on it for long when, one morning at Rocky Top, I just all of a sudden decided to shut my mouth. We was sittin at that big ol' table Miss Debbie picked out for the ranch kitchen, and I just went quiet and commenced to sippin my coffee. Mr. Ron was sittin across from me, writin everthing longhand with a pen on yellow paper.

"What is it?" he said. "You haven't shut up all morning. What's got your tongue all of a sudden?"

I didn't look at him. "I been thinkin 'bout forgiveness," I said. "And?"

"Well, there's been a lotta forgiveness in these past coupla years," I said, finally lookin up at Mr. Ron. "Miss Debbie forgave you for steppin out on her that time. And I done forgave the Man for makin me work all them years without no pay. And God forgave me of all my sins . . . "

I could see Mr. Ron noddin along, encouraging me to keep goin.

"Mr. Ron, we speaks a lot about forgiveness," I went on, "about how God forgives us and we is supposed to forgive others. But there's a whole 'nother kind of forgiveness you don't know nothin about!"

"What's that?"

"Well, you know . . . it's that statue y'all call Lamentations.

"You mean the book of Lamentations in the Bible?"

"No sir."

Mr. Ron looked at me real hard, like he was tryin his best to figure out what I was sayin. "A statue . . . ?"

"Yessiree, a statue of Lamentations."

"Oh . . . you must mean the Tower of Babel! That's kind of a statue, and it's in the Bible."

"No sir," I said. "This ain't got nothin to do with the Bible. It got to do with the Man. You know what I'm talkin 'bout. This is the Man's law that says after a lotta time has done gone by, you don't got to go back to the pokey no more for somethin you done way back in the past."

Mr. Ron started laughin then. "Oh, you mean the *statute* of *limitations*!"

"That's it!" I said. "If we gon' write this book together, I got to know *all* about that statue before I tells it all!"

It was May 1968. Now in case you ain't heard nothing 'bout Angola [Prison], it was hell, surrounded on three sides by a river. I didn't know this then, but in those days, it was the darkest, most vicious prison in America.

A few days after I got there, a prisoner I had met back at the Shreveport jail saw me and reached out like he was gon' shake my hand. Instead, he gave me a knife. "Put this under your pilla," he said. "You gon' need it."

The reason I needed to know about that statue of Lamentations was 'cause a' somethin that happened to me after I left the plantation. One time when I was a bad man, I held up a bus. Now, you might already know I had to go to the pokey for that. Ten years they gave me, and that was a long stretch. So I wadn't gon' be tellin too much more about the pokey if I was gon' have to go back to the pokey for tellin it!

It might sound strange to say this, but Angola Prison was a dynamic and precious thing. Down there in the bayou, they specialized in makin men outta boys. Funny thing about it was that even though all I did was hold up a bus, the Man decided to send me to prison in style. They packed me onto one a' them little ol' aeroplanes and flew me down. Plane landed right on the property.

Once I wound up there, the Man sent me to the worstest camp they had. They called it the "Bucket a' Blood," and I'd only been there one day 'fore I figured out why. Somebody got killed there ever night.

My first night in Angola, a great big brother came up to me and looked me up and down. "What you need from the store, man? I'm goin over there right now."

I thought maybe he'd heard about me from the fella that give me the knife in Shreveport—like maybe he was lookin out for me. So I said, "Bring me some cigarettes and two or three candy bars."

He brought 'em to me at my bunk, which was in a big ol'

buildin shaped kinda like a barn. Purty soon, I found out them things wadn't free.

That night I was layin in my bunk on my back, starin up at the ceiling. I could hear rats in the walls, and somewhere way off, a man screamed. Wadn't no lights on where I was at, and the cell was blacker than the bayou on a new moon.

"You ready?"

That big brother was standin right by my side. He'd slipped in real quiet and sneaked up to me in the dark without me even knowin he was there.

"You ready?" he said again, his voice a little lower. A little deeper. Right then, I knew what he was after.

"Yeah, I'm ready," I said. "But I got to go to the toilet first."

I swung my feet down onto the floor, and brother-man stepped back to let me get out of bed.

"You go on and lay down," I said. "Put the sheet over you. I'll be right back."

I walked away from the bed into the pitch dark. I heard a whispering sound as his pants crumpled to the floor, then a *creak-creak* as he laid down on my bunk. The toilet was on the other side of the room. I walked over there and unzipped my britches, let him hear that I was doin what I said I was gon' do.

"You want a cigarette?" I said. "For after?"

"Sure do," he said, kinda cocky. I could hear him chucklin in the dark. So on my way back across the room, I stopped at the little shelf where I had stashed my cigarettes that he'd done bought me. It was also where I'd stashed my knife.

Brother-man screamed when I stabbed him. Screamed like a woman 'cause I 'xpect I turned him into one, right through the sheet.

I bent down close to his ear and growled real low. "You or any a' your friends come 'round here again, I'm gon' finish the job."

While he was howlin and cryin and, I 'xpect, holdin what was left of his manhood, I saw lights go on outside. Then I heard boots poundin and guards drawin down. But they stopped outside the door to size up the situation.

"Moore! Who you got in there?"

"This fella's done gone crazy!" brother-man screamed. 'Cept he didn't call me "fella." "Get in here and kill him 'fore he kills *me*!"

They sent me to the hole for that. But didn't nobody try to make me his woman no more.

That's why, though, when I think about Miss Debbie reachin out to me, my chest gets tight. I had told her straight up that I was a mean man, but she didn't have no way a' knowin how mean. I thank God today she found the courage in her heart to love me enough so that someday I could tell you that even a black ex-con from Angola that stabbed a man could maybe someday do some good in the world if he gets a chance.

DON

The Art of Homelessness

Most of the thirty or so men sitting in a circle at the Union Gospel Mission in Saint Paul, Minnesota, didn't look like they'd been acquainted with a comb for a while. Their clothes were clean, Don Thomas told us, but they didn't quite fit. Some of the men were addicts and ex-cons. Some were just down on their luck. Don wasn't sure such a rough-looking batch of guys would be interested in what he had come to say.

"I'm here to see if any of you would be interested in learning a little about art," said Don, a designer for an architectural firm in Saint Paul. "Drawing, painting, that kind of thing."

Some of the men threw each other skeptical sideways glances. Others kept their eyes trained on the floor. But one man with a ruddy, wrinkled face and approximately four good teeth spoke right up. "We ain't gonna weave any of them [expletive] baskets like we did in prison, are we?"

"Oh, no," Don replied with a smile. "We're going to draw naked women."

The whole circle burst out laughing, and a show of hands revealed that every man present was suddenly, miraculously, interested in what Don had to teach about art.

I believe art can make a big difference in anyone's life. After Deborah died and Denver moved in with me, I suggested he try his hand at painting. He thought that was a good idea, judging that he couldn't do any worse than some of the multimillion-dollar pieces he'd seen by Jackson Pollack and Pablo Picasso when I took him to the Modern Art Museum of Fort Worth. And once he started, Denver took to painting like a bull rider to a rodeo. Since *Same Kind of Different as Me* came out, he has sold more than three hundred paintings.

Art had made a difference for Don Thomas too. In fact, it had been his salvation.

After his mom died when he was a teenager, his dad raised him. A proud Marine, his dad numbed the pain of his loss with alcohol, and Don was left alone a lot. "By junior high, I was making bad decisions, drinking, being cavalier about relationships with girls," Don says. "It's amazing I didn't get myself in trouble for fathering a child too young."

Fortunately, a high school art teacher reached out to the young man and helped him find a different path. "To be able to draw what I was feeling and seeing, to express some of my anger—I believe it changed my life."

Don went on to become a principal at a prominent Saint Paul commercial architectural firm while also pursuing fine art as an avocation. Every year around Thanksgiving, his firm would pass the hat among the employees for donations to the mission; then management would match those donations and write the mission a check.

But something about the way all that was handled bothered Don. "In the end, I thought it was a little disrespectful," he says. "It was like we were saying, 'We'll give you the money, but we don't want to see your people or hear about what you do.'"

So, in 2008, Don toured the mission and found himself amazed at the dedication of the staff, at the work being done. There were addiction recovery classes and classes on life skills such as parenting, budgeting, and computers. There were job skills training programs and connections to agencies that could help with transitional housing.

After his tour, Don knew without a doubt that writing a check just wasn't going to be good enough for him anymore. He had to share with these men, give of himself, make a difference.

That's when he piped up and offered to teach a class on art.

Now he found himself in a roomful of homeless men, sharing a little about his own tarnished past and how art helped him cope with the pain and heartache of his mom's early death.

"I have no clue why art works, why it helps," he told his world-weary audience. "I'm not a therapist. All I know is that it's powerful for me. And if I can give any of that to you, to be able maybe just to see the world a little differently, it will be worth it."

The following week, about a dozen men returned. One guy in the program, Dave, was a real talker. Dave liked to draw, but he liked to talk even more. He came for a couple of sessions, but after the third, he walked up to Don and said, "I really appreciate what you're doing, but I'm not going to come in anymore. I've decided to focus on another part of the program."

"Thank you for telling me," Don said, wondering whether he hadn't made the class interesting enough.

Later that day, though, one of the mission counselors told Don, "Dave's an addict. It was an enormous step for him to come and let you know his plans. Most guys in recovery just drift away."

Somehow, Don's commitment to teaching the men art had inspired Dave to honor that commitment by taking responsibility—something addicts rarely do.

Don remembers another man, Alex, an alcoholic who was extremely talented at a particular style of drawing.

After Don complimented his work one day, Alex asked him, "Do you think I could make money at it?"

"Well, your stuff looks like tattoo art," Don said. "I know a guy who gets eight hundred bucks anytime someone uses one of his drawings for a tattoo."

"Maybe I could do something like that," Alex said, adding shading to a dragon figure he was drawing.

Alex didn't come back the next week . . . or the next. Later, Don heard he'd started drinking again. Still, their conversation suggested a glimmer of hope. "Alex was looking beyond the next hour, the next drink, at what the future might hold.

When he first started teaching at the mission, Don had hoped to uncover some hidden talent—the next Picasso or Remington, undiscovered, wrapped in rags instead of a fancy art degree. Perhaps inside one of these broken men lay an artist who had only been waiting for the right nurturing.

Soon though, Don realized that it wasn't the art itself that was making a difference to these men but "the doing of the art, the stories surrounding the art."

Drawing and painting calmed the men down, helped them express themselves in a different way. "You don't have to put everything into words," Don says. "Sometimes you don't have words."

Beautiful gardens surrounded the mission—flowers, vines, and trellises sheltered in leafy canopies of shade. One day, Don took a handful of men outside and told them, "Pick anything you want to draw. But whatever you pick, you're going to draw it eight times."

It was an exercise in commitment. "Commitment and follow-through is hard for addicts," Don said. "They want something that's immediate. When something doesn't work quickly, they move on to something else."

One man picked a vine-covered trellis. But as he sketched and sketched, he focused on the trellis itself, struggling over and over to render the spots where the thin, white wood crossed. It was as though he didn't see the vines or the leaves or the flowers at all. Meanwhile, he became more and more frustrated and impatient.

"Slow down a little," Don coached him. "What else do you see here? Do you see leaves? Shadows? Colors?"

The man tried again, this time relaxing a little, sinking into the moment, less intent on the hard detail and more open to the total picture. After a few more tries, he showed his piece to Don, who was impressed with what the man had achieved in the end.

Art, said Don, teaches something we all need to learn, especially about people who are different from ourselves: "To see things the way they truly are, sometimes you have to look more deeply."

15

Ron

When *Same Kind of Different as Me* finally came out, I took Mama and Daddy a copy and wrote inside: "Thanks for being who you are. If it hadn't been for you, there would have never been me! Love, Ronnie."

Mom read the book first and declared it a literary masterpiece. Of course, my mama had also declared me handsome that time she sewed me a matching shirt and short set from blue and black plaid, a new outfit she made special for my first date with a sorority girl from Texas Christian University.

Dad started reading the book a few days later and stopped on page 18 after reading, "Somewhere during my childhood, he crawled into a whiskey bottle and didn't come out till I was grown."

A couple of days later, I pulled into their driveway. They were sitting on the porch in their wrought-iron rockers, and Mama was working a crossword puzzle.

"Why did you say what you did about me?" Daddy asked the instant I walked up.

"What did I say?" I said, knowing without asking which part he was referring to since it was about the only time I referred to him in the book.

"About me crawling in a whiskey bottle," he said, taking a sip from his Jim Beam and Coke.

From out of nowhere, my Mama cut in like a linebacker intercepting a pass. "Because it's the damn truth, Earl!"

My mouth fell open. I think it was the first time I'd heard her cuss.

Earl stuck out his chin, defiant. "Is that what you think of your old man?"

"Daddy, I've forgiven you for that," I said, without really meaning it.

"Well, I'm not gonna be reading the rest of your book," he said.

Neither, it seemed, was anybody else. When *Same Kind of Different as Me* appeared in bookstores, we thought it had *Oprah* written all over it—or at least the *Today* show, *Good Morning America*, or, as a backup, *Jerry Springer*. We thought if no one wanted to talk literature, maybe Denver could slug it out with a preacher caught in a sex sting.

But nothing happened. We sold a few copies here and there, but Oprah never did call. In fact, we dedicated a line to her from that old Randy Travis song, which said something like, I guess if my phone's not ringing, it's probably not you.

After a big Texas book fair chaired by relatives of mine refused to feature *Same Kind*, I got seriously discouraged. If you can't count on some good old-fashioned nepotism to help sell your book, what can you count on?

"Denver, what are we going to *do*?" I fumed one night as we sat on the deck at Rocky Top, watching fish pop from the Brazos River under a silver moon.

"I'll tell you what we gon' do," he said. "We gon' stop right here and bless all them folks that turned us down. They done did us a big favor. Mr. Ron, we didn't write this book for no book fair or no TV show. We wrote it for Miss Debbie, and we wrote it for God."

Then Denver pinned me with his drill-bit squint, his eyes catching moonlight. "Now, you listen to me *real good*. You hear me?"

"Yes . . ."

"Don't you never ask nobody to do nothin for this book ever again. This is *God's* book! You let Him take care a' His business, and you and me will be doin just fine. Did you hear what I said?"

In that second, I wished I had his faith—faith like I used to have. But I was afraid he might cut me with his eyes if I expressed any doubt.

"Yes, I heard you," I said.

"Then stop your complainin," Denver said. Then he turned back to watch the fish.

About a month later, we got a call asking us to appear on a morning television show in Boston. The host had read our book and taken a shine to it. A few days later at five in the morning, we sat in the studio, listening to the lead-in.

"Live in Boston, good morning!" the host said. "Today we have with us two men from Dallas, Texas, with a beautiful story about friendship."

Then he turned to Denver, who suddenly looked exactly like a rabbit frozen in the path of an oncoming semitruck.

"Mr. Moore," the host said, "can you tell us a little bit about your book?"

Stone silence.

Tick.

Tock.

Tick.

Tock.

I was about to jump in and answer when Denver spoke up. "Now, sir, I'm gon' tell you the truth. I don't read, and I don't write, so I didn't write that book, and I ain't never read it. Now, what is your next question?"

On the outside, I grinned like an idiot. Inwardly, I crumpled. My mind flashed back to Denver telling me, "This is *God's* book!"

That's a good thing, I thought, *because God help us if we ever get invited to another TV show.*

111

16

Ron

God did help us. In late 2006, as Denver and I traveled from city to city, we began to hear stories of people whom we considered our "ground zero" readers, people who picked up *Same Kind of Different as Me* and instantly grasped the simple arithmetic of Deborah's life: loving God means loving people, and loving people means making a difference for God.

Take Jill Bee from Dallas, for example. She sent the book to her friend David Smith, who lives in Atlanta. Over the next nine months, he bought sixty-five hundred copies of *Same Kind of Different as Me* and passed them out for free—seeds planted that would later yield an incredible crop. In the tenth month after reading our book, David hosted a fund-raiser that became the largest ever held in Atlanta. That gathering in the Georgia World Congress Center raised nearly a million dollars that benefited several homeless missions in the city.

Or how about the woman who checked *Same Kind* out of a public library in Syracuse, New York, because she saw it on the new-release table and liked the cover? It was a seemingly random act. But it would radically change lives thousands of miles away in the Pacific Northwest.

After reading Deborah's tale, this woman called her brother, Don, in Pasco, Washington, and told him that though she didn't go in for religion the way he did, she really enjoyed our little "God story."

Don found a copy of the book in his local bookstore and, after reading it, passed it along to his pastor, Dave, at Bethel Baptist Church. Within a week of receiving it, Dave read *Same Kind of Different as Me* two and a half times, then began writing a sermon series on compassion, forgiveness, and loving the unlovable.

Now, don't give up on this story because this next part is going to look like I'm bragging about selling a truckload of books. That's not what it's about at all, so just hang in there.

On the last Sunday of September 2006, Pastor Dave preached the first of his six sermons, telling his congregation of more than twenty-five hundred that he wanted every one of them to read his book. Within hours, his phone rang. On the other end of the line, the manager of the local Barnes & Noble said, "What did you tell all these folks about this book we've never heard of? We've taken orders for nearly a thousand copies!"

Later, Pastor Dave had another idea. He'd invite Denver and me up to Washington state to speak at his church. In a leap of

113

faith, Pastor Dave picked up the phone again and, somehow, got hold of my cell-phone number.

Fifteen hundred miles away, in a rat-shack relic of an ancient log cabin high atop a mountain near Angel Fire, New Mexico, I heard two things in rapid succession:

Ding-a-ling-ling! Ding-a-ling-ling! . . .

. . . and . . .

"Turn that thing off!"

The first was my cell phone ringing. The second was my hunting partner, Rob Farrell, who was hopping mad that I had probably just scared off the *muy grande* bull elk we'd been tracking for two days.

Embarrassed but hoping it was good news about our book, I whispered furtively into the phone. "Hello?"

"Is this Ron Hall, the author of *Same Kind of Different as Me?*" Pastor Dave said.

"Yes," I whispered.

"Praise God!" said Pastor Dave. Then, "Why are you whispering?"

"Because I'm hunting elk on top of a mountain in New Mexico," I whispered, "and we've been sitting here for days waiting to see an elk."

Not seeming to grasp my dilemma, Pastor Dave launched into a bubbly tale of what was going on at his church and invited Denver and me to come up and speak. After a ten-minute call— punctuated by Rob's angry glares and me whispering single syllables to let Pastor Dave know that Rob hadn't shot me yet—I hung up.

Rob shot me a final frown. "You just ruined our whole hunt," he said.

Five minutes later, I shot an elk worthy of the Boone and Crockett record book.

Now, here's the reason I said earlier to hang in there with me on this story. Two weeks later, I received a phone call from a woman who had been in the congregation when Pastor Dave preached his first sermon on *Same Kind of Different as Me.* For months, she said, she'd felt as if she were drowning in a swamp—a failing marriage, declining health, and a formerly vibrant spiritually life now on life support. She and her husband were living under the same roof physically, but emotionally they were oceans apart, like two rowboats bobbing in high seas at opposite ends of the Pacific. The only thing keeping them paddling was their two small children.

"My husband was clinically depressed," she told me. "The doctors didn't know why, but he was suicidal and couldn't even go to work anymore. While I went to work every day, he stayed in the bedroom with the door shut. When I came home every afternoon, I wasn't sure whether I'd find him alive."

But one day the previous week, she said, something had changed. She came home from work as usual that afternoon, but when she entered the bedroom, she heard sobbing.

The cries were coming from inside the closet.

Her first thought was that her husband had tried to kill himself but had failed. Terrified, she reached for the doorknob. Inside the walk-in closet, she saw her husband curled up on the floor among a dozen pairs of shoes. Tears streamed down his cheeks and neck, and sobs racked his chest visibly, the sound seeming to come from deep in his soul.

He raised his eyes and looked at her. "I found this book on your nightstand." He continued to weep as his wife stared in disbelief at the copy of *Same Kind of Different as Me* lying in the floor near his head. "I've been having an affair. It has destroyed my life and your life and was about to destroy our whole family. It was eating me alive, and I was so ashamed of the pain I had caused and the pain I was in that I thought it would be better for everyone if I was dead."

As I listened to the woman tell me her tale over the phone, I knew exactly how the man felt. When I cheated on Deborah, I felt as if I had ripped her apart physically. The guilt was excruciating, as though I had taken an ax to the neck of an innocent.

In my ear, the woman continued her story. As she stared at him on the closet floor, her husband had said, "Today, I read this book about how Debbie forgave Ron, a man just like me. If you will forgive me the way she forgave him, I promise to love and honor you the way he loved her."

Holding the phone to my head, I sat there astonished at the incredible chain of events that started with a woman who checked out a book in Syracuse because she liked the cover, then ended in

Washington state with a saved marriage—with an elk hunt in between. That chain of events would never have occurred if an ordinary Texas woman named Deborah hadn't decided to forgive and a man who could neither read nor write hadn't decided a book needed to be written.

Suddenly, I pictured God in heaven, all these seemingly unconnected lives unfolding under His omniscient eye, rubbing His hands together and telling the angels, "Now watch *this*!"

Two weeks after that amazing phone call, Denver and I met the woman and her whole family, who considered themselves the beneficiaries of a miracle. And I considered how, every now and then, God answers prayers for healing with dazzling, resurrection-caliber feats. But more often, He does it using humble tools, like an illiterate, homeless man and an unbelieving woman with a library card.

MANDY

The Blessing Bank

A humble prayer and a chance exchange with a store clerk put Mandy Elmore on the path to helping kids help the needy—and Mandy can't even be *around* kids. In 2008, a little boy sneezed near Mandy. Two days later, she was hospitalized, one of three times she was hospitalized that year. Mandy, age thirty-six, suffers from cystic fibrosis ("CF"), a chronic respiratory disease that puts her at severe risk of life-threatening infection.

"If I catch a cold, within two days I'll have pneumonia," Mandy told us. That means she has to be careful about contagions, which means she has to be *very* careful around kids, especially little ones who carry germs like the postman carries mail. As a CF sufferer, she can't have any kids of her own, either. And the sad irony of the whole situation is that Mandy Elmore loves kids.

"My husband, Matt, and I are kind of alone in our age group, in our community, in our world," says Mandy. "Here we are in Texas, where everyone has 2.5 kids. But we don't get to go to Little League. We don't get to trade kid stories. It's different, and sometimes it's a hard difference. Sometimes, when people are complaining about having to take their kids to Little League, it's hard for us to hear those complaints."

So it was especially hard when Mandy felt a tugging on her heart to reach out to kids. In 2007, she got the sense that God was telling her to do something for children. "But I didn't know what. I can't have kids, I can't even be around kids. I didn't know what I was supposed to do."

Then a friend, Mary Lynn, gave her *Same Kind of Different as Me.*

After reading about Deborah Hall's commitment to the homeless, Mandy knew she, too, wanted to make herself available for whatever God wanted her to do. Knowing she wanted to make a difference for kids, but not knowing how, she cried out to God in prayer. "Whatever You can do to help me find my purpose, Lord, just lead me," she prayed. "Let me fulfill Your purpose and, in doing so, be fulfilled. I know I'm here for a reason. Just show me what to do."

In October, the Lord did just that. Mandy and Matt were doing some Christmas shopping for family when she saw what she thought was a child's bank with a cross on it. But when she asked the store clerk to show her "that cross bank," he said, "No: that's a cross, and that's a bank. They're two separate items."

Like sheet lightning brightening an evening sky, inspiration lit Mandy's mind. She turned to Matt. "I know what it is!"

"You know what what is?" Matt replied, his face a question mark.

"I know what we're supposed to do!"

In that moment, Mandy's purpose arrived in her mind fully formed. "We're supposed to make banks that teach children to give to others!"

Before the night was through, Mandy and Matt had gone home and searched the Internet, looking to see if anyone was already doing what Mandy wanted to do. When they didn't find anything, Mandy went to the craft store and returned with an armload of balsa wood.

"I didn't even know what balsa wood was," she says. "I am the least creative person on the planet."

For the next three days, Matt watched in wonder as Mandy designed and constructed four banks for children. She worked well into the night, burning with a conviction that she knew what her message was. It was the same message her own father had passed to her: to give to others freely. The banks would be a special place for children to set aside money to give to people in need. It was Matt who came up with a name for the project. They'd call the little boxes "Blessing Banks."

"If we couldn't have children of our own, maybe we could help other parents teach their children to live lives of compassion," Mandy remembers.

In November 2008, Mandy began telephoning manufacturers of wooden toys and other products and telling them about her vision, hoping to find a way to mass-produce her banks. After all, who would want a balsa bank?

One company she contacted was the largest manufacturer of toy wooden trains in the country. The man on the phone listened kindly as Mandy told him about her balsa prototypes. Then he tried to let her down easy. He thought the Blessing Banks were a great idea and was sure Mandy's heart was in the right place, but he already had too many customers and more work than he could handle. Still, just to be nice, he agreed to take a look at her balsa creations.

"I sent him the four banks, and I sent him the book," she said, referring to *Same Kind of Different as Me.* She also sent him a note. "Read this book and be inspired," it said. "You never know what God has in store for us."

Then Mandy gathered a group of friends to pray that this very successful businessman would somehow be moved to work with a Texas woman who knew nothing about business at all.

Six weeks later, Mandy's phone rang. She's still not sure whether it was the businessman who read the book or his wife. But when he called in January 2009, he told Mandy, "My wife is a cancer survivor. She was very interested in Deborah Hall's story, and she says I'm crazy if I don't do these banks."

Soon an acceptable prototype was complete, and within weeks the Blessing Bank was ready for market, complete with a prayer card suitable for the simple kindness of a child: "Dear Lord, thank You for blessing me. Please help me use this bank to bless others."

Mandy and Matt opened a Web site at www.blessingbanks

.com. Slowly the banks began to catch on, and parents began calling to report the impact of the banks on their children.

In Connecticut, a young girl's best friend lost her home in a fire. The girl saved all her money in her Blessing Bank and gave it to her friend.

In Dallas, one child is filling his Blessing Bank with money to buy shoes for kids in his city who have none.

An El Paso boutique owner called Mandy to tell her that she was buying Blessing Banks in bulk to sell in her store. Her young son, she said, had never expressed an interest in saving money before, but after his mom bought him a Blessing Bank, he asked if he could do chores around the house so that he could earn money to fill it. But the chores weren't filling the bank quickly enough to suit him, so he decided to sell rocks. And when they heard *why* the boy was selling rocks, people actually bought them.

"The little kids get it," Mandy says. "All it takes is a heart for giving."

17

Denver

I had known Mr. Ballantine when he stayed at the mission. Sometime before Deborah and I started serving there, Denver told us, he had watched a car screech up to the curb on East Lancaster. The driver shoved an elderly man out of the passenger-side door, pitched a beat-up Tourister suitcase out behind him, and roared away. Abandoned on the curb, the old man staggered like a drunken sailor on shore leave and fired off a salvo of slurry curses. But to Denver, he also looked . . . scared. At the time, Denver had still been an island, a stone-faced loner who didn't poke about in other people's business. But something—he thinks now maybe it was how helpless the old man looked—plucked a string in his heart.

Denver walked up to the man and offered to help him get into the mission. In return, the man cursed him and called him a nigger.

I'd been livin with Mr. Ron for a good while when I got a call from some lady said she was a nurse. Said she was takin care of my friend, Mr. Ballantine, at a gov'ment nursing home. He wadn't doin so well, she said, and didn't have too much longer to live. Mr. Ballantine had told her he wanted to see me one last time.

I had known Ballantine from the first day he came to the Union Gospel Mission. He wadn't no volunteer. His son had drove up to the curb in a car, put Ballantine out on the sidewalk with no more than a suitcase, and drove off like bank robber leavin the scene of the crime. That was the last time Mr. Ballantine ever saw anyone in his family.

He was purty old, in his eighties, and he couldn't get around real good, and didn't nobody like the man 'cause he was as mean as a cottonmouth snake. Matter a' fact, the first time I tried to help him was that very first day when his son put him out of the car.

"Here. Let me get that for you," I said, reaching for his beat-up ol' suitcase.

"Get the hell away from me, nigger!" Mr. Ballantine said. He sprinkled a few other words in there I won't put in this book.

But something about that ol' man made me want to help him. He couldn't get around too good, and it was tough for him to come down to the dining hall at the mission, so whenever I got my plate, I took one to him too. Ever time I did, he called me a nigger, but I just figured that's the way he was raised up. He didn't mean nothin by it. 'Sides, a man's got to eat.

After his health got real bad, Mr. Shisler said they couldn't take care of Mr. Ballantine at the mission no more, so they moved him to a nursing home that was just about as nasty as you could get. I remember that time when Mr. Ron's friend brought Mr. Ballantine some cigarettes and Ensure, and he said to me:

> *"Why would that man buy me cigarettes when he doesn't even know me?"*
>
> *"'Cause he's a Christian."*
>
> *"Well, I still don't understand. And anyway, you know I hate Christians."*
>
> *I didn't say nothin for a minute, just sat there in a ole orange plastic chair and watched Mr. Ballantine lyin there in his bed. Then I said to him, "I'm a Christian."*
>
> *I wish you coulda seen the look on his face. It didn't take but a minute for him to start apologizin for cussin Christians all the time I'd knowed him. Then I guess it hit him that while I'd been takin care of him—it was about three years by then—he'd still been callin me names.*
>
> *"Denver, I'm sorry for all those times I called you a nigger," he said.*

I told Mr. Ballantine that it was okay, and he stopped calling me nigger that day.

Well, now they'd moved Mr. Ballantine again, that nurse on the phone said, and then I went to see him. The new place was near downtown Fort Worth, across the tracks from the mission, and it wadn't too much better than the old place. The attendants didn't do much for him 'sides drop his food and leave.

His cancer had gotten real bad, crawled down his throat and was eatin up his tongue, the nurse had told me on the phone. I went on up to the floor where they said his room was, and when I walked in, Mr. Ballantine was sleepin. I didn't say nothin, just stood real quiet at the foot of the bed. He was nearly naked, covered in just a bedsheet, and that was soiled. Thick nails covered his bony ol' toes like potato chips. His old gray head was greasy, and his hair stuck up from his head in patches like scrap cotton.

I didn't think he even knew I was there, but all of a sudden Mr. Ballantine spoke up. "Well, Denver . . . glad to see you."

His voice came out raspy, like his mouth was full a' sand or steel wool.

"How you doin, Mr. Ballantine?" I said.

"I'm not doin so good, Denver. Don't have much time left. Not much time at all."

"You all prayed up?" I asked. I had taken Ballantine to church, and he'd liked it, but I didn't know if he'd ever done business with the Lord.

"Well, I'm not sure about that," he said, turning a little in his bed and motioning me over. "But I did want you to know how much I appreciated you looking out for me, bringing me food at the mission, and all that. You were a real friend to me, Denver— about the only one I had."

126

I walked over beside the bed and looked down at Mr. Ballantine and saw a broken-down man. I thought about his son, dumping him on the curb like a piece a' trash. I thought about how he had at one time been somebody's son, somebody's true love, somebody's husband. Now here he was, about to die, with nobody but a sorry fella like me to say good-bye to.

"Mr. Ballantine," I said, "I didn't do nothin for you that somebody else hadn't done for me."

"Well, that may be so, Denver, but you were about the only person who showed me love when I wasn't very lovable. I just wanted you to know that I didn't forget."

Then Ballantine got a twinkle in his eye. "Denver, there's something else I need to tell you," he said.

"Yessir?"

"You're *still* a nigger!"

We laughed together until Mr. Ballantine broke down coughin, then purty soon he quieted down and looked at me real serious. Finally, he closed his eyes and slipped away. I was honored to be there to see him on through to the other side.

JOSHUA

Dirty White Spot

Joshua Plumley doesn't want to write a book or become a famous painter. "If I wanted to do that," he says. "I'd go to an art gallery or hunt down that John Grisham guy."

So instead, Joshua wrote us a letter—a letter about the struggles of race.

"I can imagine telling my wife the choice I made to write y'all like this," the letter said. "Silence and a stare would be her response, her way of telling me she loves me but figures I operate on half a brain sometimes."

But Joshua was compelled to write, he says, having grown up a "dirty white spot" in Birmingham, Alabama.

"I spent all my time with black kids," Joshua says. Growing up in the shadows of the civil rights movement, "I never knew that skin color meant God either liked you or didn't."

As a matter of fact, Joshua remembers that the best time he ever had growing up was when he and his friend, Melvin, would collect pine cones, like soldiers stocking an ammo depot, and fire them, like grenades, at squirrels.

But the whites in Birmingham looked down their noses on such things. The general opinion seemed to be that if a boy was going to harass woodland creatures, that was fine and well. But he ought to do it with someone of his own race.

"The day a white woman asked me why I was wasting time with the black kids haunts me still," Joshua says. And that was in the 1980s.

Years later, Joshua married an African-American woman. Then in 2002, he wore out the knees of his jeans in turbulent prayer with God over his mother's battle with cancer.

"Kill the cancer!" he would pray. "Don't take my mom away!"

His mom's name is Debbie.

"When God chose to heal my mom, I started believing in miracles," Joshua says. "Maybe I would have seen more if I hadn't waited so late to start believing. It's a shame so many people die lonely and tied up with hate. I figure now, at twenty-nine years old, one of the biggest reasons people miss the face of Jesus is because of how they hate the color of someone else's skin."

18

Ron

Eighteen months after *Same Kind of Different as Me* came out, I took a copy of the Sunday *New York Times* to share with Mama and Daddy. Miraculously, our book had made the bestseller list.

"Is this some kind of joke?" Daddy said. "Why would anybody want to read a book about you and Denver? Y'all ain't nobody, and you sure ain't no John Grisham!"

I swallowed my irritation. "You're right, Dad. We are a couple of nobodies. But the good news is, we were loved by a real somebody named Deborah."

Then it really hit me. Apart from Deborah's love and Christlike forgiveness—forgiveness I didn't deserve—Denver and I would have never had a story to tell. She threw my sin as far as the east is from the west and never mentioned it again. For twelve years, not a day passed that I didn't think about what I'd done. I don't know if she did or not, but never once did she even insinuate that she remembered.

I don't believe my dad ever did anything intentionally to hurt me the way I did to Debbie. And yet for sixty years, the equivalent of a life sentence, I had withheld love from him because of my unwillingness to forgive him. Sure, I had done nice things for him and Mama. On the surface, I had acted the part of a good son. But in so many small ways I had punished him, discriminated against him for his weakness. Deborah had quickly forgiven me much, yet I had held on to my resentment, unwilling to give it up. It was my turn to let go of my grudge and really forgive him, though he didn't deserve it, and not beat him over the head with it ever again.

That day, I invited my daddy to spend a couple of days at Rocky Top, just the two of us. He packed an overnight bag and grabbed the Stetson I had given him the Christmas we bought the ranch. We sat on the patio and watched wild things cross the river and the eagles roost in the big cottonwoods. When the stars came out, I built a fire, opened a bottle of cabernet, and lit two Davidoff cigars. We toasted and reminisced; he began crying; then I did too.

He told me about his grandfather, a drover born in 1860 who made the first of many trips up the cattle trails when he was just fourteen. Frank Hopson was a cowboy and horse trader who had lived in Hamilton and Hico, towns just thirty miles from where we were sitting. Frank was my great-grandfather, Mama Clara's daddy I'd never heard about. The three sisters and Dad had taken care of him for the last twenty years of his life until he died in 1937. I missed knowing him, but as a kid, I dreamed of being a cowboy just like him. That night, looking over the Brazos with my daddy, I met Frank Hopson for the first time.

"This is the best day of my life," Earl said to me that night, his voice breaking with sobs. "I'm eighty-nine, and I never thought I'd ever get to have a drink with you!"

It felt good. It felt right.

Then, as the fire slowly simmered down to embers, my daddy began to recite poetry. First Longfellow, then Robert Frost's "The Road Less Traveled." The moment surprised me. I had never thought of him as being interested in literature or culture of any kind. But his recitation was brilliant—perfect in pitch and rhythm. No wonder his old buddies had loved drinking with him; the old man was smart and funny.

I read him a poem I'd written about my granddaddy, my mother's father, Jack Brooks. I call it "Boots Too Big to Fill." He cried, not knowing how much I had loved his father-in-law. He'd never really gotten to know him. (Granddaddy didn't drink either.)

"Write a poem about me," Earl said that night.

And I will, though it hasn't come to me just yet. Over a bottle of wine and two cigars, I met my father on his terms. And for the first time in my life, I liked him.

We talked about Jesus. My brother had prayed with him fifteen years earlier to receive salvation. Daddy said he believed he still had it. I do too. We prayed again, thanking God that it was a gift not to be taken back.

After midnight, the fire went out. We sipped the dregs of our drinks, and I helped him to his room.

"This has been the best day of my life!" he declared again.

We finally agreed on something. It had been one of the best days of my life too.

That Christmas, I gave my daddy a gallon jug of Jack Daniels Black Label. He cried once more. "It's the nicest present anyone gave me!"

That was saying something since I'd remodeled his whole house, bought him all new furniture, and given him a Jeep Grand Cherokee just a few years ago! But he was so proud of that bottle of liquor. He called all his friends and neighbors to come see his "Black Jack" displayed on the coffee table like a Henry Moore sculpture. In his mind, it was way too valuable to drink. He never opened it but kept it on display. After all, it was his favorite gift ever. He had just turned ninety.

19

Denver

When I was just a little fella, folks said there was a man named Roosevelt who lived in a white house and that he was tryin to make things better for colored folks. But there was a whole lotta white folks, 'specially sheriffs, that liked things just the way they was. Lotta times this was mighty discouragin to the colored men, and they would just up and leave, abandonin their women and children. Some was bad men. But some was just ashamed they couldn't do no better. That ain't no excuse, but it's the God's honest truth.

I thought Lupe Murchison's house was big, but I hadn't never seen nothin like that place where the president and his wife lives at. It was never in my mind or my personality that I would ever wind up at the White House. It was never even my desire. So when me and Mr. Ron rolled up to the gates in a dark blue limousine, it was like bein' in a movie.

Mr. Ron and I was invited to eat lunch with the Bush family right in the upstairs part of the White House. It was a part of a celebration of reading that the president's mama was in charge of. I guess she's purty big on readin. Well, we drove 'round a driveway in the shape of a circle and rolled up to some doors guarded by Marines. They were lookin mighty sharp in their uniforms, which was the same color as the car. We got out the limo, and I never did see one of them fellas so much as bat an eyelash. I was glad they's on my side.

Once we was inside, we went into this fancy room that Mr. Ron said was where the diplomats come to. It was a mighty nice place with lots a' big ol' paintins of old-timey men on the walls. With all them rugs and flowers and big ol' sparklin lamps, the place reminded me of that Worthington Hotel in Fort Worth where I went and accepted that award for all Miss Debbie's hard work. When I was sleepin on the heatin vent out behind the hotel, I never did 'xpect to go in that place either.

Now here I was at the president's house, and we was s'posed to meet up there with some other folks that wrote some a' Miz Bush's favorite books. Purty soon they started to come in. One of 'em was Marcus Luttrell.

Mr. Ron said this fella was a war hero in Afghanistan who had earned a Navy Cross. I was honored to be there with him.

He came in as a guest with a lady that turned out to be married to the governor of Texas.

"I want you to sit by me at lunch, Denver," she said.

A coupla other writers came in, too, and I got introduced to em. Jim Nance, a sports fella from TV, was one of 'em. He had written a book.

We got to go on a little tour of the place, even walked right by the president's office, and then we went to the private elevator that the president hisself uses to go upstairs to get some sleep or get hisself somethin to eat. Along the way, I seen some men in suits with wires stickin outta their ears. They was nice enough, but I could tell if I'd a' looked cross-eyed, they'd a' taken me down to the fancy carpet with no questions asked.

Ron went up first 'cause the elevator could only take a few people at a time. Then I rode up, and when the doors opened, there was these two white ladies just a-smilin at me.

"Denver Moore!" said a lady with silvery hair and a necklace around her neck. "I am so glad to finally meet you! Can I have a hug?"

I didn't know whether I was s'posed to do that since I had had a lot of trouble with white ladies in my life. But Mr. Ron leaned over and said, "It's okay. That's Barbara Bush, the president's mother." So I walked over and gave Miz Bush a hug. She smelled like flowers.

There was another lady standin there, too, and I had seen her on TV enough times to know that she was Laura Bush, the president's wife.

Then one of 'em said to me—I can't remember which one—that she was proud I'd learned to read and write. That's somethin I been workin on the last coupla years. And I don't know that I'm proud, but I got to admit it makes gettin 'round town a whole lot easier.

Laura Bush said her husband, the president, was gon' come up and join us, but he was tied up with somethin right then, and did we want to go out on the balcony for a little snack?

While we was walkin out there, Mr. Ron told me we was in the "residence," the part of the White House where all the presidents have lived. And when we got out on the balcony, there was one of 'em sittin right there! It was Miz Bush's husband, the *first* President Bush. He was mighty nice to me.

Out there on the balcony, it was a warm spring day, and we could see that great big flat pond and that famous statue that points up to the sky like a giant railroad spike. I sat down at a table, and some waiters in bow ties started comin 'round with trays full a' food I seen at some a' them fancy places Mr. Ron dragged me to. But I was too nervous to eat much 'cause I was afraid them teeth Mr. Ron had made for me might fall out. It had happened before, and I didn't want it to happen in front a' no president!

Well, we sat out there sippin our drinks until Miz Bush asked if we'd like her to show us around the place. I 'specially remember two places she took us. One was the president's private office. He had a TV in there, and I 'xpect he could sit down in there and watch some baseball if he wanted to. The most amazin thing about that office was the desk. Miz Bush told us it was the desk where President Lincoln hisself had signed the Emancipation Proclamation all them years ago. I thought that was really somethin—that I would be standin there, a black man, the great-grandson of slaves, now a guest a' honor in the White House, standin here lookin at the spot where a great man signed the paper that set my family free. It was somethin I never woulda dreamed of.

Next place we stopped was in the Lincoln bedroom. I swear everthing in that place was gold! Gold curtains, gold carpet, gold chairs. There was even a giant golden crown over the top of the bed. I was standin there tryin to keep my mouth from hangin open when I heard Laura Bush speak up. "Well, hi, sweetheart. I'm so glad you made it."

I turned around and wadn't lookin at nobody but the president hisself.

George W. Bush walked right up to me and stuck out his hand. "Denver Moore! What an honor to meet you, sir."

Well, I felt like I had to be dreamin now. Here was the president of the United States of America, treatin me, a poor homeless man off the street, like I was some kinda important person. I didn't know what to think. I don't even remember what I said back to him . . . somethin 'bout bein glad to meet him, too, I imagine. But

I shook George W. Bush's hand, and I ain't the smartest fox in the barnyard, but in that handshake I felt like a whole lotta history passed through: croppin all year just so I could pay the Man, passin by water fountains where a colored man couldn't get a drink, and spendin most a' my life bein called a nigger. Bein dragged by my neck behind horses when I was sixteen years old. Scratchin and scrapin and bathin in fountains in Fort Worth. And now here I was, an ol' 'cropper with a prison record, shakin hands with the most powerfulest man on the earth.

Ain't nothin that can do somethin like that but love. The love Miss Debbie had for the homeless had carried me all the way to the White House. And while the president still had ahold a' my hand, God reminded me of that scripture where He says, "Through Me, all things are possible."

All things. Did you hear me?

The president was a real Texas fella like Mr. Ron, wearing boots and a cowboy belt with his suit. I liked that. Made him seem kinda regular.

Next thing Mr. Bush did was walk over to that war hero fella, Marcus, and I remember exactly what he said. He said, "Marcus, when I gave you your medal, I gave you my phone number and told you you could call me anytime, day or night. You put your life on the line for our country, and I want to do whatever I can for you. You haven't called me. I want you to call me."

Marcus smiled and was mighty humble. "Yes sir, I've got your number, and I know I can call if I need to."

Well, we got finished lookin at the Lincoln bedroom and walked out in the hallway again and looked the place over some more. The president hung around with us for 'bout thirty minutes. Him and Mr. Ron knew some of the same folks in Dallas, and I heard 'em talkin about how Mr. Ron and Miss Debbie used to sit behind the Bushes at the Texas Rangers game when Carson and Regan and the Bush girls was little and Mr. Bush owned part a' the team.

Purty soon this other fella came out and told us, "Lunch is served," and we all marched into a fancy dining room. The president couldn't stay with us for lunch. Laura Bush said somethin had happened in one of them foreign countries, and he had to go tend to it.

Well, lunch came. I don't remember what they served exactly, but them waiters in black bow ties brung us lots a' different plates, a little a' this and a little a' that. I liked the food purty good, but I was still mighty worried about my teeth.

Someone introduced me to the president's brother and sister. There was another lady there that had wrote a book, and I remember it because I liked the way the title sounded: *The Glass Castle*.

All them folks was real nice to me. When it got near the end of the meal, I thought it'd be polite to say how much I appreciated it, so I got everbody's attention. "I want to thank all you folks for invitin me here today," I said. "It's the greatest honor of my life. I wish I could thank you all by name, but to tell you the

140

truth, all you Bushes look alike. Matter a' fact, all you white folks look alike."

I was just tellin it like it was, but I still thought Mr. Ron was gon' have a heart attack.

Lookin back on that day, I can't hardly believe I had lunch at the White House sittin between Laura Bush and the governor of Texas's wife. I didn't know whether to be happy or scared. It kinda reminded me a' that time when Miss Debbie and all them white ladies was sittin outside the mission in Miss Debbie's car, tryin to get me to go up to that Christian "retreat." 'Course, this White House thing was just one meal, with just *two* white ladies to sit between. I thought I could handle that better than goin up to the mountains with a whole carload a' white ladies and them wantin to cry and pray over me.

'Course, if I hadn't gone to that retreat and had so many folks prayin over me, I might not have ever been sittin there at the White House. I had gone from livin in the bushes to eatin with the Bushes, and I know a whole lotta prayer went into that.

CARMEN

Bossy White Lady

I was hopin God had done broke the mold for bossy white ladies when he made Miss Debbie. But that was about like hopin Oprah Winfrey was gon' ask me to marry her, and sho 'nough, I met Miss Carmen Brown, this lady on the radio down there in Florida. Miss Carmen is on a show called *The Morning Cruise with Dave, Bill, and Carmen.* She looks like a white man's dream, and I ain't gon' say she was my nightmare, but I will say she pushed me way past the limit on my comfortability.

First thing she did was float me and Mr. Ron up all across Florida on her radio show, like one of them hot-air balloons. Then she and her radio friends started up a great big bicycle ride to raise money for the homeless and got folks from all over the state to join in. I'm tellin you the truth, that lady can talk to a stump and make it listen! She been talkin 'bout me and Mr. Ron on the radio for more than two years now, and ain't no sign of her shuttin up.

I learned a lot from knowin Miss Carmen—geography and stuff like that. First time me and Mr. Ron went to Florida for a visit, we was havin us some breakfast down by the ocean. Now, I ain't gon' lie, I was tired of Mr. Ron draggin me all across the country. I asked him, said, if he was such a good businessman, why didn't he take care a' all our business the first time we was here so we wouldn'ta come back to the same place?

Mr. Ron looked at me over his coffee. "Denver, this is our first trip here," he said.

"It sure ain't!" I said. "I remember sittin right here by the water that don't stop just a couple a' months ago."

"Denver, that was California. We're in Florida, all the way on the other side of America, three thousand miles away."

Well, my eyes got pretty big then. "Mr. Ron," I said, "you mean to tell me that Florida went and got themselves a ocean too?"

That wadn't the last time I seen the ocean in Florida 'cause Miss Carmen invited me to come back again and again. Fact is, if I answered my phone ever time she called, she'd have me busy till the Lord came back to claim me.

One day in 2007, she bought me a ticket on a aeroplane and showed up at the airport to get me. And there she was, this blonde white lady drivin this flashy white-on-white-in-white foreign somethin-or-other. She wrapped me up in a hug like I was family. Color didn't matter to her, but it did to me. My mind just kinda went back in time to the trouble I'd had with white ladies—like that time I tried to change a flat tire for one of 'em and wound up with a rope around my neck and white boys holdin the other end. I was scared, real scared, like a brother at a Klan rally. Then Miss Carmen pushed a button on the dash, and the whole top a' that car come off and slipped down in the trunk. And there I was, sittin in the front seat of that white lady's white convertible, and me stickin out like a hunk of coal in a snowbank. But Miss Carmen was real proud, and she drove me around town like I was one a' them famous astronauts comin home from a moonwalk.

Now, bein in radio, Miss Carmen knows lots a' famous singers. I ain't really no singer, and I told her that, but that didn't matter 'cause she's like Miss Debbie. When I say I can't do somethin, she don't listen. Before I knowed it, Miss Carmen had done flew me up to Nashville and introduced me to lots of famous singers, like Chris Tomlin. I even got to do a little singin with 'em.

After I got back to Texas, Miss Carmen showed up *again*, this time at Mr. Ron's ranch takin lots of pictures, askin too many questions, and bossin me around just like Miss Debbie did, thinkin she was gon' make me be her best friend. I guess she did a purty good job 'cause today Miss Carmen is 'bout the best white lady friend I got.

20

Ron

By the end of 2007, Denver and I had crisscrossed the country dozens of times, speaking at least 250 events. I got so busy on the road, trying to change the world, that I never considered the possibility that I was as broken and needy as the homeless people I championed.

After nearly a hundred events during the first five months of 2008, I retreated again to Italy. I landed in Pietrasanta, an artists' colony and the destination of great sculptors who for centuries went, and still go, to carve the famous Carrera marble. One evening I was enjoying a Cuban cigar and a local wine made from Tuscan grapes with a cadre of international artists when my phone rang.

It was my mama. Dad had fallen. Mom had called 911, and the ambulance had already whisked Dad away to North Hills Hospital.

"Come home, son," she said, sounding at the end of her rope.

"Your dad's asking for you. He's driving me crazy, and I'm praying he doesn't make it."

From anybody else, that might've seemed callous. But Tommye Hall had put up with a whole lot of grief from her husband over the decades. She was getting old, and I couldn't blame her for wanting to leave this earth with a little peace and quiet under her belt.

I hopped the next plane out of Rome, but Dad still beat me back from the hospital and was at home when I arrived in Haltom City. He was back up, ornery as usual, and complaining about the cost of the ambulance. "Tommye shouldn't have called the ambulance; she should have called the neighbors! There wasn't nothing wrong with me except I couldn't get up!"

Then he said in that joking way that lets you know a person is at least half serious, "Maybe your mother and I will just move in with you. I'll bet it's lonesome in that big ol' mansion with just Denver and you."

I laughed and asked him if he was trying to audition as a stand-up comic.

Later that week, I was sitting on Mama and Daddy's porch, talking with a longtime neighbor, David.

"I hate to tell tales out of school, Ronnie Ray, but I'm worried about your daddy," David said. "Earl gets in his truck several times a day and lights out for who knows where. And whenever we ask him where he's been, he can't remember. Only time anybody knows for sure where he's been is when he comes back carryin a fifth of Jim Beam."

I glanced over at Dad's little red pickup sitting in the driveway. I knew he hadn't been sliding over to the Tailless Monkey since it had been shut for at least twenty years.

David looked me right in the eye. "He's gonna kill somebody, Ronnie."

I agreed.

That day, I confiscated my parents' car keys. Mama took it in stride. Daddy screamed like a panther and fought me to get them back. "I ain't never had no wreck or no ticket!" he hollered.

I looked at him and said, "Dad, that's God's mercy, defined."

That night, he fell again. Mama called 911 again. After a few days at North Hills, I moved him to Life Care Center of Haltom, a nursing home. He wouldn't have accepted that from me, but his doctor didn't give him a choice.

I checked him into his room, which had two beds, one of which was empty. That was a good thing since a roommate would've given Daddy an accomplice in planning an escape.

Earl looked at Jerri, the head nurse, a fiftyish blonde, and said, "Honey, I gotta have at least two Jim-Beam-and-Cokes before dinner—not too much Coke—and a cigar for dessert."

Jerri, who might've been a pageant queen in her younger days, had the sweet smile of a caregiver and the eyes of a drill sergeant. "You try that, Mr. Hall, and you'll be out on the street."

For the next three weeks, during what must have been basically detox for him, Daddy called me at least ten times a day.

"Why'd you leave me here?"

"Come get me!"

"If you love me, you'll bring me some whiskey!"

I thought about that. The man was ninety years old and had been pickling his innards since before I was in Little League. He was at least ten years past being sent away for treatments and didn't have much longer to live. Why make him spend his last weeks in misery?

So what the heck. I bought him a large Coke at a Sonic drive-in, poured out half, and filled her up with Jim Beam.

When I arrived at the nursing home, Daddy was sitting in a wheelchair beside his bed, watching TV.

I held out the Sonic cup. "Here, you want a Coke?"

He waved me off. "Nah, I don't want no Coke."

"You better take a drink of it before you turn it down."

I handed him the Coke, and he took a sip. A big ol' grin blossomed on his face; then tears blossomed in his eyes. "You really do love me," he said.

A few days after I took Daddy the loaded Sonic Coke, I moved Mama in with him. It turned out he hadn't needed an accomplice, and every time the nurses weren't looking, he had tried to make a break for freedom on his own.

After sixty-five miserable years of marriage, Mama did not

go willingly. But she finally agreed to occupy the other bed in the room.

My telephone rang at two the next morning. "Ron, there's an old woman in my room that's been chewing my ass out all night!" Dad warbled into the phone. "I haven't done nothing to her. No sex, no nothing—hell, I ain't even kissed her, and I ain't goin' to! Can you come down here and make her leave?"

"An old woman?" I said, ribbing him a little. "Who in the world is it?"

"Hell, I don't know who she is!"

Then from across the room, I heard Mama yell, "I'm your wife, you ignorant bastard!"

Then, in my ear: "She says she's my wife, but that ain't right. I don't know *who* she is!"

It was just like home.

The fighting raged for days, rocking Life Care like a rickety rowboat in a thunderstorm. Then one morning about three weeks later, the director called me.

"Mr. Hall, I'm sorry to tell you this, but we've had to evict your father." She then described a pattern of domestic quarrels, escape attempts, and all-around unruliness. "I'll need you to have him packed and off the premises by sundown."

I was irritated because moving Dad was definitely going to be a pain in my butt. Strangely, though, a note of pity sounded in my heart. When applied to my daddy, it was still an odd, foreign sound. But it was not unlike the compassion I felt for so many of the homeless men and women I'd been trying to help over the last eleven years.

Sure, many of them had made their own beds in life and, as a result, had wound up sleeping in rags under a bridge. But Denver had taught me that to love a man enough to help him, you have to forfeit the warm, self-righteous glow that comes from judging.

I had developed quite a do-gooder reputation for myself by refusing to judge "bad sorts"—bag ladies and vagrants, drug addicts, drunks, and runaway teenagers who sold their bodies for money.

Strangers.

But I was just now learning to do it for my own flesh and blood.

I had no doubt that an ornery cuss like Daddy deserved to be tossed out on his can like a drunk—like when Mr. Ballantine's son pushed him out of his car, motor still running, on the curb in front of the Mission. I had all this compassion for Mr. Ballantine, but it had taken me all this time to muster up compassion for the man who gave me life. And more than that. Earl Hall had been an alcoholic absentee father, crappy husband, and all-around curmudgeon, no question. But he had provided for his family for sixty-five years, which wasn't true of many of the homeless I'd reached out to.

As a boy, I never missed a meal. I had a roof over my head, a cosigner for my first car. And Daddy had never asked me for money except in joking, and that was after I remodeled his house and he knew I was stacking it up.

Dad's drinking never caused him to miss a day of work. Now he was an old man, his body failing, mind not far behind, with a wife who loathed him and a son who for most of his life had held him at arm's length with nose pinched, as though holding a dirty diaper. A troublesome thought formed at the edge of my mind: was I so shallow, my do-gooding so superficial, that I could only set judging aside and help a person as long as his sins didn't affect me?

21

Denver

One day, I asked Mr. Ron, "Mr. Ron, all these white folks be invitin us to their Bible studies. How come none of 'em's invitin us to their Bible doins?"

I ain't sayin it ain't all right to study the Bible. You got to study the Bible to know the rules of life. But I notice a lotta folks doin more lookin at the Bible that doin what it says. The book a' James says, don't just *listen* to what God has to say, *do* what He says. And Jesus said God is gon' separate us, the sheep from the goats, based on what we *did*, not on how much we *read*.

I was havin a conversation 'bout this with this smart fella I know named Mike Daniels. I says to him, "How anybody gon' know, Mr. Mike?"

"How anybody gon' know what, Mr. Moore?" he answered.

"How anybody gon' know God when all the time folks got their head stuck in a book? I can talk to you 'bout this stuff,

Mr. Mike, and you won't get mad, but some folks thinks I'm a bad man or is blasphemin or somethin, but I ain't. It just seems like lots of folks is tryin to pull God outta somethin or someone, and that ain't never gon' happen. You know what I mean, Mr. Mike?"

"Yes sir," Mr. Mike said. "I believe I do.'"

"How we gon' really know God if we trying to get Him out of a man or woman? How we gon' know God for real lookin for Him in some kinda religion, in some kinda system? I don't mean know *about* God, Mr. Mike. I mean really, honest *know* who God is?

"Mr. Mike, so many folks is tryin to get to God and know Him by *doin* somethin, like tryin to make a deal with Him. Thinks if they does somethin for God, He'll turn 'round and do somethin for them. Thinks that we is all way down here, and God is way off yonder someplace far off outta reach. Most people thinks that we all got to get a education or study all the time, *then* we know, but that just ain't so. It ain't so at all."

"You're right, Mr. Moore. That ain't so. That's not the way it works, not even a little bit."

"Mr. Mike, everbody's lookin for God everywhere on the outside. He ain't in no book, and He ain't in no preacher, and He ain't in nothin or no one on the outside. You got to go inside 'cause that's where God is—in the deepest place inside you. And ain't nobody gon' make God tell you nothin. Ain't nobody gon' have no wisdom 'bout nothin if they thinks they can read 'bout it or hear about it from some man or woman. That got to come from revelation. That got to come from the Holy Spirit inside us, Mr. Mike, and that ain't somethin that can be bargained for. You can't achieve revelation. You can't work for what's free."

Since I been visitin a lotta churches, I hear people talkin 'bout how, after readin our story, they felt "led" to help the homeless, to come alongside the down-and-out. But when it comes to helpin people that ain't got much, God didn't leave no room for feelin led.

Jesus said God gon' *separate* us based on what we did for folks that is hungry and thirsty, fellas that is prisoners in jail and folks that ain't got no clothes and no place to live. What you gon' do when you get to heaven and you ain't done none a' that? Stand in front a' God and tell Him, "I didn't feel led"?

You know what He gon' say? He gon' say, "You didn't need to feel *led* 'cause I had done wrote it down in the Instruction Book."

Let's be real. A lotta folks on the list that Jesus calls "the least of these" ain't the ones you gon' find down at the country club. No, most a' them's the folks you gon' find in the jail or in the street. But we got to go to *all* the people—the rich, the poor, the lowdown, and the dirty—and show 'em all we got the same thing for ever one of 'em: the love a' the Lord.

I think part a' this problem is that too many folks ain't ready to face up to the fact that to love the unlovable, they got to face people that they fear. They is afraid to get out of their regular livin space 'cause they afraid it might be suicide, am I right?

'Cause you wouldn't be scared a' nobody if you didn't feel like they was gon' do you wrong.

Most people want to be circled by safety, not by the unexpected. The unexpected can take you out. But the unexpected can also take you over and change your life. Put a heart in your body where a stone used to be.

22

Ron

The Life Care director gave me the name of the only nursing home in that end of town that would take my dad, a lockdown facility for geriatric troublemakers. I checked him in that afternoon. Just after midnight, a nurse called to tell me Dad and his roommate had gotten into a food fight that devolved into a fistfight. I tried to picture two old farts pelting each other with strained peas and tapioca, then circling each other like a couple of WWF wrestlers with their skinny butts hanging out of their hospital gowns.

"We moved your father to solitary confinement," the director said.

I went to visit him the next day and saw that he had a black eye.

I tried to talk to him, but he cursed me. A week later, I took

Regan and my two-year-old granddaughter—Earl's *great*-grand-daughter—to see him. They brought him homemade cookies. He slapped away their offerings and cursed them. Silently, I asked God to take him before I started hating him again.

A few weeks later, on Christmas Day, I took Mama to see Daddy. Last time they'd seen each other, they'd turned their nursing-home room into a war zone. As I guided Mama into Daddy's room, I braced for a hostile reception.

But I was shocked when Earl said, very sweetly, "Oh . . . Mama. Come give me a kiss."

I helped her over to his bed, and she bent down and kissed him on the lips.

"I love you, Earl," my mama said.

"I love you, too, Tommye."

The moment was as rare as a da Vinci painting.

I sensed it was the last time they would ever see each other, and I was hoping to hear them reminisce about the good times, about what had sparked their love so many years before. But it seemed they couldn't remember, or they just wanted to forget everything but this moment. There was nothing left to say, so they simply stared into each other's eyes.

Driving Mama back to Life Care, she told me about how, in October 1942, she had ridden the bus home to Blooming Grove, Texas, from Denton, where she was a junior at the North Texas State Teacher's College. Her daddy—and my granddaddy,

Mr. Jack Brooks—ran a cotton farm in Blooming Grove, and he was the hardest-working man I ever knew.

When she got home that October, she told her daddy she was fixing to marry a soldier who had just shipped off to Phoenix—Earl Hall. Never one to pass up a chance to teach a lesson about hard work, he told her that if she'd help him pick a bale of cotton, he'd buy her a train ticket to Arizona. Five days later, she'd picked her bale, and her daddy drove her to the train station.

Listening to Mama tell this tale as we drove through Haltom City, I still couldn't trace the roots of her love for Earl Hall. "So why'd you marry him?" I said.

She laughed. "Because it beat pickin cotton!"

So there I had it. I owed my very existence to my mother's aversion to the cotton patch.

CAROLYNE

Not Just a Pretty Garden

Thirteen years ago, Carolyne Snow set aside a career working for entertainment mogul Barry Diller to become a full-time mom. Still, she and her husband, Robbie, a music marketing executive, kept in touch with entertainment industry friends. One of them was Mark Clayman, producer of *The Pursuit of Happyness*, the 2006 movie starring Will Smith.

In May 2008, during a visit to the Clayman home, Mark gave Carolyne a copy of *Same Kind of Different as Me.* By then, Mark had already optioned the book for film. Still, he regularly passed along the book to friends.

"Read it," he told Carolyne. "I want to know what you think about it."

Not only did she read the book; it set her to work on a project that is still underway.

The plight of the homeless had torn at Carolyne's heart when she traveled to downtown LA in the predawn hours to visit the commercial flower market there. "I exit at Sixth Street and head down to Maple," she says. "You notice the people with cardboard boxes wrapped around them and see tents set up all along the street."

The police allow the homeless to pitch these makeshift

bedrooms by night but require that they clear out by six in the morning. "So many people say, 'Oh, well, these people are just drunks and addicts," Carolyne says. "But I remember one morning when I saw a mom and her small children packing up their stuff. As a mom, I can't imagine what that would be like. I wondered what this woman must have suffered in her life to arrive in that position. It was heartbreaking."

The Snows live in Santa Clarita, a small town just north of Los Angeles. While there is very little homelessness there, there is a large Hispanic community pocked with poverty. After reading *Same Kind of Different as Me*, an idea began taking shape in Carolyne's mind: a community garden with beds set aside to grow produce for food pantries serving the homeless and the working poor. She envisioned a garden that could not only provide nutritious food to people who needed it, but that could also attract children to a service project and teach them the value of sowing and reaping, literally, in their own community.

"I felt this was something I could do that would bring people in and involve them without being churchy," Carolyne said. "I'm not really a 'religious' person. Spiritual, yes. Organized religion, no."

But starting a community garden turned out not to be as easy as finding a vacant plot of land and diving in with roto-tillers. The logistics of involving children in the project required that the garden be centrally located. As the idea developed, it made the most sense to launch the garden at a public school.

Carolyne's research led her to a Los Angeles—based group called the Garden School Foundation, a group that in 2003 started a prototype garden at central LA's Twenty-Fourth Street Elementary School, an institution where 100 percent of the students come from homes with incomes low enough to qualify for free school lunches. The Garden School Foundation's philosophy is that "schools should be like parks, not prisons; the best way to learn about good food is to grow it; and children have to know nature to love it."

Carolyne went to visit the prototype garden, which included neatly cultivated rows of vegetables, a garden shed, and straw paths meandering through the plot. "The kids working in the garden were so polite and so respectful," she remembers.

When Carolyne commented on the children's behavior, the man in charge told her that the students were what is known in "educationese" as "at-risk" kids—that is, students from extreme poverty, whose neighborhoods were riddled with gang activity, crime, and drugs.

Carolyne, from the upscale suburbs, observed the kids' model behavior and tried to imagine the kinds of homes they went home to at night. "You could see the value of this project to them," she said. "You could see that the garden was providing something for these kids that went beyond health and nutrition and what's taught in a science class. It gave them someplace to go, a sense of community, a purpose."

After visiting the Twenty-Fourth Street school, Carolyne headed back to Santa Clarita with a clarified purpose of her own. She wrote a proposal for her own school-based community garden that would not only serve the poor but also tie in with California education standards. "It's not just a pretty garden," she says. "A lot of research has gone into it."

At this writing, Carolyne is lining up funding for the garden, which she hopes to launch during the 2009–2010 school year and provide free produce to two local food banks. While she has volunteered in the past at a community hospital and with the PTA, her introduction to another side of Los Angeles has enriched her world and brought out in her a new compassion for the poor.

"There's a little bit of Deborah in all of us," Carolyne says, "if we'll just let it be there."

23

Ron

Spending hours each week captive in a kitchen that smelled like rotten eggs boiled in Pine-Sol was bad enough. But I fervently did not want to be touched for fear of the germs and parasites I suspected floated in every particle of the air.

Chef Jim and Deborah chatted easily while I mentally balanced the ledger between pleasing my wife and contracting a terminal disease. I had to admit that his idea seemed like an easy way to start—serve the evening meal once a week, and we'd be in and out in three, four hours max. We could minister from behind the rusty steel serving counter, safely separated from the customers . . . The whole arrangement seemed like a good way for us to fulfill Deborah's desire to help the homeless without our touching them or letting them touch us . . .

n early 2009, Denver and I were invited to speak at a fund-
raiser on the campus of an affluent college situated, postcard
perfect, in the middle of an immaculately groomed Norman
Rockwell town. Board members for the city's homeless shelter
were trying to raise money to complete construction of a new
facility. It was an invitation we'd turned down a number of times
due to scheduling conflicts, but the people who ran the shelter
kept after us.

"Our shelter is in terrible condition and has been for years,"
the director told me, "but the city won't get behind us. We need
someone to come and help."

Finally, it worked out that Denver and I could say yes.

Our talk was scheduled for late in the day, so we first paid a
visit to the shelter the director had said was in such bad shape. By
then, Denver and I had traveled to more than two hundred different homeless shelters and programs in towns across America.
But never had we seen anything like this.

Typically, cities stash their homeless in the ugliest building in
the ugliest part of town, but this shelter was an absolute disaster.
Situated in a rundown old storefront in an abandoned part of
town, the mission was smack up against the railroad tracks. The
dilapidated structure had to be at least fifty years old, and it
appeared not to have seen a coat of paint since it was built.

Inside, we saw thirty-eight men stacked like galley slaves in a
dimly lit room large enough for three. Scanning the room, I saw
mix-and-match bunk beds lining the walls, which were stained

with a collage of what appeared to be urine, smoke, and vomit. The mattresses on the beds looked as though they'd been recovered from a bomb site.

Denver and I exchanged glances, and I could read his eyes. He'd never seen anything worse.

Down a hallway, the floor of which was lined with patches of green linoleum that peeled away to reveal rotting plywood underneath, were equally luxurious bathroom accommodations: one commode and two showerheads for all those men. Looking at the grime embedded where grout used to be, I concluded that there hadn't been a can of Lysol in the building since the days they cooked it in kettles. As Denver and I moved to the dining room, I looked up to see that the ceiling was bowed and caving in.

I had seen the homeless living in burned-out buildings and cardboard boxes. But I had never seen them living in worse conditions in a facility that purportedly had not only volunteers but also a purpose and a goal and a budget. In fact, the only thing this shelter had going for it was walls and a roof to keep out the cold. Even then, Denver said, he'd rather have slept under a bridge.

Later that day, Denver and I spoke to a crowd of seventeen hundred people, which included everyone from the governor's wife to judges and state representatives—cream-of-the-crop citizens from the city and the state. Never had I lit into an audience before, but what I had just seen made the skin on the back of my neck burn.

"The whole world knows who you are," I said. "You have a great, world-class university here. You have nationally ranked sports teams. But you have the last-place homeless shelter. Of the more than two hundred we've visited, it's the worst in America we've seen. As proud as you are of your city and the university, this is how you treat your homeless people?"

I wanted to ask how many in the audience had ever been to the shelter to lend a hand. But I didn't because the shelter director had already told me the answer: fewer than 20.

I then quoted from Matthew 25, which says Jesus will judge the nations based on how they treated "the least" of "these brothers of Mine":

All the nations will be gathered before Him; and He will separate them from one another, as the shepherd separates the sheep from the goats; and He will put the sheep on His right, and the goats on the left. Then the King will say to those on His right, "Come, you who are blessed of My Father, inherit the kingdom prepared for you from the foundation of the world. For I was hungry, and you gave Me something to eat; I was thirsty, and you gave Me something to drink; I was a stranger, and you invited Me in; naked, and you clothed Me; I was sick, and you visited Me; I was in prison, and you came to Me." . . . The King will answer and say to them, 'Truly I say to you, to the extent that you did it to one of these brothers of Mine, even the least of them, you did it to Me."

I pointed out to my audience the little catch in Jesus' words: *"to the extent that* you did it to one of these brothers of Mine."

"If you thought Jesus was coming to your shelter today, would you have left it in that condition?" I asked. "Guess what? Jesus is at your shelter every day, and He doesn't like the way it looks and smells."

That night, the city raised eight hundred thousand dollars toward completion of the new shelter. After the talk, a woman walked up to me, her face flushed with embarrassment. She was the wife of the board member who was raising the money.

"I'm so ashamed to tell you this," she said. "My husband and I have served on the board of the shelter for years, but I've never been inside. I didn't realize how bad it was." The closest she had come to actually helping the homeless in her town, she said, was dropping off old clothes on the shelter doorstep.

"The good news is that you're doing something about it now," I told her.

That woman's former attitude—and her present shame—reminded me of no one more than my sorry self. I know what it's like to "help" from afar, to do some throwaway, feel-good gesture like giving away some clothes I didn't want anyway or to go through the backbreaking labor of scribbling out a check. Before Deborah dragged me down to the Union Gospel Mission, the last thing I wanted to do was get my hands dirty.

I remember the first time I went down to the mission with Deborah to volunteer in the kitchen. One of the first people we met was Chef Jim, a sixty-five-year-old former head of catering for an international hotel chain. After Jim's son died tragically, his wife wound up in a mental institution. Chef Jim drowned his grief in twin rivers of alcohol and drugs and wound up homeless. Now he was cooking at the shelter while he worked at rebuilding his life.

Chef Jim and Deborah hit if off right away. But while they yakked in the mission's greasy kitchen, I was calculating how quickly we could dish up some grub for the vagrants, then get the heck out of there. I was willing to help the homeless, as long as I didn't have to actually interact with them.

On and off for eighteen years, Denver had slept on the sidewalks by the Worthington Hotel, which was probably two hundred feet from my art gallery. Not once when I saw homeless people did I offer them a penny or a cup of water. I felt that any contact with these down-and-outers would be a smelly, unpleasant encounter at the very least.

Before meeting Denver, I thought of the homeless as trash on the street and prayed that our city officials would find a Dumpster large enough to hold them. My art gallery had been robbed by a couple of nasty derelicts, so I felt sure all homeless people were cut from the same ragged cloth and would probably rob me too.

Deborah and Denver changed that thinking though it took a while. They taught me not to ask myself what would happen to me if I stopped to help someone in the street but to ask myself what will happen to them if I don't?

24

Denver

This fella I know that had done been in the military once told me that when a soldier or sailor gets kicked out of the military for bad behavior, they call it a BCD.

"What that really means is Bad Conduct Discharge," this fella told me. "But what we call it is getting the Big Chicken Dinner."

Well, over in Seattle, one of them folks that Mr. Ron calls a "ground-zero reader" *gave* a big chicken dinner to a homeless fella like me, and it changed his life forever. I don't know how, but somehow a copy of our book worked its way across Washington state from Pastor Dave's church in Pasco to a little town near Seattle. The woman that got it had a eight-year-old son. She wadn't no religious woman. But after she read our book, she told her boy, said, "The next homeless person we see, we're going to help them."

Of course, she didn't know there's a difference between helpin and blessin—that blessin means you give a person a little gift to show 'em you think they matters on this earth, and helpin is when you stoop down with a person and stay there till they can climb on your shoulders to get up. Didn't matter 'cause the important thing was, this lady's heart had been touched.

The very next day, she and her boy were comin back home from the grocery store with one of them chicken dinners that's already done cooked. When they pulled into the alley next to their house, the boy seen two homeless fellas diggin in the trash. Now, I'm pretty sure they wadn't pullin the hamburger drop 'cause ain't no sense in that if you doin it where nobody can see you and give you a dollar.

The little boy, he says to his mama, "Let's give them the chicken dinner we just bought at the store!"

So they did, and they watched as them two fellas sat down in the alleyway and had themselves a feast—a Big Chicken Dinner of a different kind.

A few minutes later, back at their home, that woman began to experience what she calls a strong "impression." Now, like I said, she believed in God in a real general way, but she was not a religious woman. But she said she felt something inside her heart leadin her the way Christian folks might describe being led by the Holy Ghost. Whatever it was, she began diggin in her purse for some cash to give to them fellas that was still outside enjoyin their Big Chicken Dinner.

She came up with forty dollars, and she couldn't even believe she was about to give it over to a pair of raggedy-lookin hobos. But like she told us, she couldn't help it. So she and her son went back out to the alley and handed each one of them fellas a twenty-dollar bill.

Now, I is a expert, and I can tell you that there ain't hardly *no* homeless folks that *ever* has nobody hand 'em no twenty-dollar bill. Them fellas must a' thought they won the lottery that day.

But listen at what happened a few months after that. The woman and the little boy was at home, and here come a knock on the door. The woman put her eye up to the peephole and seen this nice-lookin, clean-cut gentleman standin on her front porch.

"Hello, ma'am," the man said when she opened the door. "Do you know who I am?"

"No sir," the woman said.

"I'm one of the two homeless men you gave a chicken dinner and twenty dollars to awhile back. Can I come in and tell you how you changed my life?"

The woman was purty nervous about lettin a stranger in, and to tell you the truth, she prob'ly shouldn'ta done it. But she was thinkin to herself how different he looked, and besides, how in the world could he know about the Big Chicken Dinner and the lottery money if he wadn't who he said he was?

The woman decided to welcome him into her home; then she called her son into the livin room to hear what this fella had to say.

"You know what I did with that twenty dollars?" he began.

She smiled, expectin him to say that maybe he'd bought the nice clothes he was wearin. "No, what?"

"I took it straight to the closest bar and got drunker than Cooter Brown!"

That's exactly why I don't give money to the homeless! the woman thought. But after she got over her shock, she remembered that this fella looked a whole lot different than what he had that day in the alley, so she decided to listen to the rest of his story.

"While I was at the bar, I met a woman that worked there," he told her. "No one in as bad shape as me had ever been in that place before. Well, her curiosity got the best of her, and she asked to hear my life story. I told her I'd been homeless on the streets for more than twenty years."

The woman in the bar asked this fella about his family.

"They think I'm dead!" he said.

The bar woman was shocked. "That's not fair to your family," she said. "You have to let them know you're still alive!"

"You don't understand, ma'am. I've done so many bad things, they'd never want to see me again. In their minds, I'm better off dead."

See, that's the thing about doin all them bad things. After you done 'em, you pretty sure you done used up all your chances with anyone that ever loved you. But that ain't always true.

That night, the woman at the bar talked that fella into goin back to his family to see if maybe it wadn't too late. At midnight, she put him in her own car, drove him down to the bus station, and with her own money, bought him a one-way ticket and put him on the next bus home.

Reminded me of the good Samaritan, using his own money to help out a poor fella he ain't never seen before while everbody else—includin the religious folks—was satisfied to pass on by.

The Seattle woman and her little boy listened to the man they had blessed with twenty dollars finish tellin his story.

"My family treated me like the prodigal son!" he said. "They were so happy to see me. I spent three months at home, and they forgave me and loved me sober. I'm still in recovery, but I've got a job and a future. And I just came back to thank everyone who helped change my life.

"Your twenty-dollar blessing was the seed money God used to turn me around," he said. "I was going to use it to drink and forget my troubles, but God used it to help me remember He still changes lives, even the lives of drunks in bars."

I was sho 'nough happy to hear that story 'cause it shows that even if you bless some needy person just a little bit, God might use other folks down the line to weave your little gift into a bigger blessin. And if you bless folks, you gon' get the blessin back, no matter what they does with the money. So you give the gift with no strings attached, and let God take care a' business on the other end.

25

Ron

Denver spoke slowly and deliberately, keeping me pinned with that eyeball, ignoring the Starbucks groupies coming and going on the patio around us. "I heard that when white folks go fishin they do something called 'catch and release.' . . . That really bothers me," Denver went on. "I just can't figure it out. 'Cause when colored folks go fishin, we really proud of what we catch, and we take it and show it off to everybody that'll look. Then we eat what we catch . . . in other words, we use it to sustain us. So it really bothers me that white folks would go to all that trouble to catch a fish, then when they done caught it, just throw it back in the water" . . .

Denver looked away, searching the blue autumn sky, the locked onto me again with that drill-bit stare. "So, Mr. Ron, it occurred to me: If you is fishin for a friend you just gon' catch and release, then I ain't got no desire to be your friend . . . But if you is lookin for a real friend, then I'll be one. Forever."

eading into 2009, I had noticed a trend in the cities we visited. Almost every one of them has a strategic "ten-year plan" for ending homelessness. These plans usually involve building more housing (as though the problem is that there are more people than buildings) and more government facilities for the treatment of addiction and mental-health issues (as though there aren't already enough programs).

Don't get me wrong. I'm glad the problem of homelessness is on the government's radar. It's just that the problem of homelessness will never be solved by government. That's because government can put a roof over a man's head and food in his mouth and even give him a job. But government can neither love a man nor lovingly hold him accountable. The chronically homeless, whether homeless through tragic circumstance or through messes of their own making, have a whole constellation of inner issues that food, shelter, and a paycheck won't fix.

Like Denver says, "If folks like me had the ability to do what folks like you be tellin us to do, we'd a' already done it."

The chronically homeless need love, compassion, accountability, and someone to come alongside them and hold them steady as they limp along the winding, pitted road to wholeness.

After I'd encountered several ten-year plans that were already on year two or three with no real progress, I began to ask two questions of people who attended our *Same Kind of Different* events: "How many homeless are in this city?" and "How many churches are in this city?"

Interestingly, most of the time there are more churches than homeless. And if you count synagogues, temples, mosques, and other communities of faith with a spiritual mandate to care for the poor, the number of cities in which the faithful outnumber the homeless is likely near 100 percent.

After I ask audiences the question about the number of faith communities versus the number of homeless in their city, I present to them what I call the Thirty-Day Plan to End Homelessness. It goes like this: How about if your pastor or rabbi or priest or imam motivates his or her congregation to adopt one chronically homeless person. Each body of believers, whether it's fifty or a thousand strong, would assume collective responsibility for taking in one person and loving that person back into society.

Let's pretend for a moment that this person's name is Joe and the body of believers is the First Baptist Church ("FBC"), a congregation of three hundred people. The first order of business would be, of course, to befriend Joe. Bless him with a few dollars, take him to coffee or maybe a meal here and there— always in pairs, in public, and never in a way that could physically endanger church members, of course. While some members of the church do this work of outreach, others could check Joe's background. In a church of three hundred, there are likely law enforcement and social services personnel who could make sure Joe is not too dangerous a character to take under the church's wing.

I want to be clear about this: loving people does not mean

ignoring realities on the ground. Remember the woman in ~~Seattle~~ Denver told you about who invited a formerly homeless man, a stranger, into her home and was blessed? Deborah and I did the same thing, and it changed our lives. But you can't go down that road blindly. Some homeless people really are dangerous.

Last year, a young man in Dallas who had decided he was going to help the homeless started working in the inner city. One day he offered a homeless man a ride in his car, and the man killed him. In another case, a wealthy woman picked up a vagrant and offered him work in her home. When they got to her house, he stabbed her.

So it's important to realize that for every man reformed after being treated to twenty bucks and a Big Chicken Dinner, there is another hard case. Does that mean every homeless person is likely a killer? Absolutely not. But it does mean that those who reach out to the homeless, many of whom are mentally ill, should exercise caution.

I remember one time when I was out in the 'hood, talking with some of the homeless fellows I'd gotten to know. I was leaning up next to a vacant building, shooting the breeze, when the other guys spotted a familiar face sneaking around the corner.

"Watch out!" one of them said. "Here comes ol' Devil Woman." Within seconds, a filthy woman in flashy clothes appeared before us like an apparition, rasping at us in a deep, gravel-filled voice that didn't sound like it could possibly belong to her. I later told Deborah she sounded like the devil himself. Ol' Devil Woman was petite and might even have been attractive except for the drug craze she was manifesting.

She leaned into my face. "I-was-a-schoolteacher," she said in a rapid-fire jive. "Who-you? Who-you? Who-you?"

That scared me so bad I wanted to jump and run. But strangely, her fast jive talk drew men like a homing signal, and she captivated them with flattery, hoping one would reward her with a free fix. "Eeeeew, ain't-you-handsome? Ain't-you-handsome? Bet-you-could-take-care-a-me-*real*-good."

I warned the homeless friend I had gone there to talk to—who was trying to stay sober and get off the streets—not to fall under her spell.

He laughed and assured me, "Ain't no way!"

Sensing the presence of evil, I slipped away and headed home.

A few days later, while dishing out spaghetti at home, we heard my friend was in jail. Ol' Devil Woman had apparently awakened some old demons in him. I heard the two of them had been arrested only a couple of blocks away from where I last saw them. She was in the hospital near death from stab wounds, and he was in jail for attempted murder, the consequences of drug addiction.

Denver is a civilized fellow now, but I remember that for months when I first knew him, I thought he might kill me. Deborah and I actually broke a cardinal rule of mission volunteering when we gave Denver our phone number and told him where we lived. Thanks to Deborah's boldness and heart, it turned out well for us and for many others who have been touched by our story. So I would never counsel you to hold back from helping out of fear. Just remember what Jesus told His disciples when He sent them out to reach the lost: "Be wise as serpents and harmless as doves."

But there's another side to this safety issue—because while FBC is carefully gauging whether Joe is a safe person to be around, Joe is watching to see whether FBC people are safe themselves. Will they catch and release him? Will FBC come on strong at first, then gradually slack off until Joe only sees them on holidays?

Homeless people are used to people who "help" with one hand and hold their noses with the other. They are used to catch-and-release friends, who feel warm and fuzzy and compassionate for a few days or weeks but then abandon their efforts when the going gets tough or when the busyness of their own lives takes over.

Will FBC be faithful to tend their relationship with Joe? Will they keep his confidences as he confesses the hardship and/or wrongdoing that put him on the streets? Joe will be watching for the same thing every other human being watches for before committing to a potentially life-changing relationship: trustworthiness.

Once the relationship is established, is it possible that FBC could go the next step and get Joe off the streets? Could he stay in a room at the church? Could FBC members chip in twenty dollars a month apiece to rent him a room elsewhere? What about food?

Can the FBC women's ministry—or the men's group—stock the refrigerator wherever Joe is staying?

"Well," you might be saying, "none of this requires Joe to do anything, to accept any responsibility."

Exactly! What FBC is offering Joe is unconditional love. Part of real love is loving a person from dependence to independence. But if that is to come, it will come in time. What the Joes of the world need first is a taste of dignity, someone to love them enough to take a chance on them.

Is it possible that Joe will freeload for a while, take advantage of the situation, then split? It's not only possible but likely, at least for a little while. The chronically homeless are often addicts, petty thieves, and practiced at the art of the small con. You don't survive on the streets by being an upright citizen.

But if Joe turns out to be unable to follow through on real change, that's fine too. FBC has done what God called it to do. Jesus said we will be judged by how we treat the hungry, the thirsty, the prisoner, the stranger. We are judged by *our* compassion, how we live *our* lives, not by how Joe ultimately lives his. God commands us to love, not to calculate the end game. It is only when Joe is loved without strings that he is set free to (eventually) turn a corner and voluntarily become accountable to those who have placed faith in him.

Moving on in the thirty-day plan, think of the no-cost resources available in a single church. Doctors who can provide medical care. Licensed counselors who can provide mental-health

assistance. Teachers who can help Joe brush up his reading, writing, and math skills or help him study for his driver's license exam. Social services workers who can help Joe secure the essential documentation he needs and navigate intimidating places like the social-security office, county clerk, and the most terrifying place of all—the Department of Motor Vehicles.

Here's something else a community of faith can do that the government can't: give Joe a job. While I was walking the streets of Fort Worth, I ran into former chefs, construction workers, personnel managers, auto mechanics, executives, skilled military technicians, and stonemasons like José. Homelessness does not confine itself to the unskilled. In a single church, there are bound to be people who, if they can't employ Joe directly, know someone who can. If there aren't, maybe Joe would be willing to do general maintenance of the church facility itself, paid for out of the church's mercy fund or by collective, specifically earmarked contributions of members.

If one person tried to take on Joe, the task would be daunting, overwhelming, as I can tell you from experience. But many hands make light work. And within each body of believers, there are endless caregiving possibilities that, unlike government programs, can be customized according to need. You see, in this case it really does *take a village*.

So far I haven't heard of any takers on my thirty-day plan. I chalk that up to two very human factors: excuses and fear. When I first started going to the mission with Debbie, I was far too busy to go—in my own mind, that is. I had plenty of excuses not to go: teenagers to tend, art to sell, clients to schmooze, accounts to manage, and many, many toys that clearly needed use and maintenance. I only went with Debbie because I wanted to be a good husband, having been such a lousy one years before.

Even then, I was afraid. Of being somehow victimized. Of being stabbed, maybe, or shot—or only robbed if I was lucky. While Debbie chatted with Chef Jim during our first trip to the Union Gospel Mission, the list of rashes, bugs, and parasites I just knew were ready to attach themselves to me out of thin air rivaled the entire database at the Center for Disease Control.

Today, I'm so glad that guilt overcame my fear and that Debbie's passion for the poor eclipsed all my arrogant and convenient excuses.

Denver says, "You got to stoop down to help a man up." But after the homeless began to bless me much more than I blessed them, after my heart started to warm to the task, I realized that God didn't command us to love only for the sake of others but for our own sakes as well.

MICHAEL

Entertaining Angels

This fella named Michael from Waco, Texas, wrote to us after he read our story, said he used to be pretty hard on homeless people. Now he's takin a homeless man to church. It's kinda sad, though, 'cause Michael says the other folks in the church look at him and his homeless friend like they is a coupla skunks.

That's what he says: "Skunks."

Ain't that somethin? I guess some folks still thinks people got to clean themselves up on the outside before God can get busy cleanin up the inside. That ain't true at all. God *specializes* in turnin trash into treasure.

Michael said his new homeless friend don't trust the folks in the church, but that he is startin to trust Michael, went out to breakfast with him same as that time I went to that restaurant with Mr. Ron for the first time. Putty soon, Michael says, this homeless fella started openin up with his story. After that, one a' Michael's friends told him, said maybe that homeless fella was Jesus in disguise.

That might not be far off the truth. Jesus said whatever we does to the lowliest people, it's like we done it to him. And remember them angels Abraham entertained? They looked

183

like your everday strangers, just some stray fellas travelin on down the road. But Abraham and his wife went on and treated 'em like honored guests. We needs to take a lesson from that. You never know whose eyes God is watchin you through. It might not be your teacher, your preacher, or your Sunday school teacher. More likely it's gon' be that bum on the street.

26

Ron

A week after Christmas, the nursing home staff told me Daddy was going down fast. On the third day of January 2009, after an hour-long meeting with hospice, I said, as gently as I could, "Daddy, you understand, don't you, that you don't have too much longer on this earth?"

"Hell, yes!" he said. "I'm ninety-one years old, I got cancer, and I can't eat, but you ain't talkin to no dummy!"

"How about the two of us going for one last hurrah?" I said. "You just tell me where you want to go and what you want to do. Your wish will be granted, just like on that old TV show, *King for a Day.*"

Dad didn't hesitate. "Take me home," he said. "I want to sit out on my porch, drink good whiskey, and smoke cigars."

Of course, every one of Dad's requests, from going off the grounds without permission to ingesting harmful chemicals,

broke most of the rules posted on the board at the nurses' station. However, I figured that for an old bird about to take his last
flight, rules were meant to be broken.

Working quietly, I helped him into a wheelchair. Then I
opened the door to his room, wheeled him casually past the nurses'
station and out the front door, triggering an alarm that sounded
like I'd just touched off a three-engine fire.

Dad just smiled and waved *adios*.

"You're gonna get your ass in deep trouble, Buddy-roo," he
said as I loaded his skinny butt into the front seat of my Range
Rover.

I smiled slyly. "Do I look like I care?"

"No," he allowed.

"Do you care if *I* get *you* in trouble?"

A great big grin split his wrinkled face from ear to ear.
"*Hell*, no!"

We laughed like Butch and Sundance on the edge of that cliff
just before they jumped.

Steering the Range Rover one-handed, I punched up my
brother, John, on my cell phone and told him to meet us at Daddy
and Mama's house. Then I called the neighbors I'd known most
of my life. "I'm bringing Daddy home for a last hurrah. Y'all come
on over and say good-bye." On the way home, I stopped at a
tobacco shop and bought five Romeo and Juliet cigars.

When we pulled up to the house, I carried Dad up to the
front porch and set him in his wrought-iron rocking chair. As

the neighbors started to filter over, I ducked inside to look for his whiskey.

I didn't have to look far. Right there in the front room, in the middle of the coffee table, like the centerpiece at a holiday banquet, sat the gallon of Jack Daniels Black Label I'd given Daddy for Christmas the year he turned ninety.

No reason for him to keep saving this now, I thought. I stepped into my parents' tiny linoleum kitchen to rustle up an icy glass of Coke, then broke the seal on the Jack and poured my dad a drink.

On the porch, we lit up our ten-dollar cigars and remembered: the West Fourth Street slums . . . donkey basketball . . . the time a runaway horse pitched Daddy over a fence near the creek where we used to go crawdad fishing . . . and that feisty little Rusty Fay who used to ride down the street in a halter top on the back of her wrestler husband's Harley, driving all the neighborhood men wild whenever the bike hit a bump.

Earl's eyes grew warm and misty, whether from wistful reminiscing or the Jack Daniels, I wasn't sure.

"Boys," he said, "I'm proud of you."

John and I exchanged glances, telegraphing our surprise over hearing our daddy finally say something we'd longed to hear all our lives.

David, the neighbor who'd ratted Daddy out for taking mysterious truck trips, ambled over. Leaning up against a porch post, he said, "Earl, you made it to ninety-one, and you're sitting on your front porch with your two sons, sipping whiskey and smoking cigars. It couldn't get no better, could it?"

"It damn sure could!" Daddy said, smiling mischievously.

David's eyes widened. "How?"

"Ronnie could've dropped me off at a wild sex party!"

We all cracked up.

Looking across the street, I saw Mama and Daddy's neighbor of fifty-seven years emerge from her little clapboard house to see what was going on at the Halls' place. I stood up and walked over to greet her.

Louise, a former hairdresser and reformed smoker, had blue hair and a gravelly voice that reminded me of a frog speaking through a bullhorn. Pushing ninety herself, she still went down to the senior dance at the VFW every Monday night. During the years of my parents' physical decline, Louise faithfully took them loaves of fresh-baked banana nut bread.

I met her in her yard. "Louise, I brought Dad home for probably the last time," I said, nodding toward the group on the front porch. "You've been such a sweet friend to him and Mama for all these years. I want you to know how much I appreciate it, and if there's ever anything I can do for you, you just let me know. I'll do anything you ask."

Louise broke out in a sly grin. "Ronnie," she rasped, "there is one thing you can do."

"You name it."

"Well, you can let me run my fingers through your hair," she said with a wheezy giggle. "I ain't touched a man's hair since Frank died in '76!"

I laughed and bent over at the waist. "Get after it, Louise!"

She reached out and got a double handful and, squealing like a schoolgirl, started rubbing both sides of my head like she was shampooing one of her weekly customers back in her salon. I laughed till I cried. Then she went over and told my Daddy good-bye.

Earl held court on the porch for a couple more hours, spinning tales and reminiscing as the afternoon sun turned the air gold. Around four o'clock, he fell silent for a few minutes. Then, in a somber and final tone, he announced, "I'm ready to go home."

"Does that mean you're ready to die?" I joked.

"Hell, no! I'm ready to go back to the nursing home and take a nap!"

Just after midnight, a ringing phone roused me from sleep. "Your father took a long nap this evening, and when he woke up, he tried to escape," the head nurse told me. "He made it about ten feet; then he fell."

His left femur was shattered, she said, and he had busted his head open, had a nasty cut above his eye. I didn't feel guilty, but I did wonder if it would have happened if I hadn't contributed to his delinquency.

"We've called 911 and are sending your father to the hospital," the nurse told me.

During a four-hour surgery, doctors at Harris Methodist Hospital inserted a steel rod into Daddy's leg. At the time, I wondered how much good it would do and whether they might be unwittingly aiding and abetting future escape attempts. But Dad did not awake from the anesthesia that day. Or the next. When he didn't wake up on the third or fourth day, I knew Earl Hall had made his last prison break.

Regan and Carson had come, and we all prayed over Dad. We gave him over to God and reminded Him that Daddy had prayed the sinner's prayer once and that we thought he had meant it. Tears spilled down my cheeks, and I felt something for my father that I hadn't felt since I was a little boy—real love.

On the fifth day, the ICU doctor came in and after examining Dad told us he only had a few hours left. The kids and I kept praying, sending him home with messages to heaven.

At about three o'clock on the fifth afternoon of his near-comatose slumber, Earl Hall suddenly awoke. I stood up and grabbed his hand. "Dad, we nearly lost you! Your oxygen level dropped below what it takes to live."

"Well, that's a damn lie!" he said, instantly Earl again. "I knew exactly what I was doing—just resting. Hell, I feel fine. Now, take me home!"

Three days later, Daddy's oxygen count fell again, and I was there to tell him good-bye.

Two days later, we buried him in Mt. Olivet Cemetery in Fort Worth, in a plot he'd owned for forty years. At his funeral service, friend after friend of Daddy's surprised me by coming up to tell me how proud he was of me.

"He said you were a famous author, like that John Grisham fella," one of his old buddies told me.

Even if I'd seldom heard such words of parental pride from Earl Hall's lips, I'm glad he thought them in his ornery old heart. At that moment, I vowed never to withhold kind words from the people I love. And I was glad I had found a way to love and honor my daddy on that front-porch afternoon, sipping good whiskey and smoking Romeo and Juliet cigars.

27

Ron

My New York partner, Michael, had called and asked if he could come see Deborah, and was on his way down. I had tried to discourage him and others from coming during these last weeks. Deborah had wasted away so that she barely raised the sheet that covered her. Her eyes had faded and seemed cruelly suspended in sockets of protruding bone. I wanted everyone to remember her as the beautiful, elegant woman they'd always known . . .

But Michael pressed, and . . . I said yes. Jewish by birth, he was not a particularly religious man . . . When Michael pulled up to the house at around 10:00 a.m., Mary Ellen and I were in the bedroom with Deborah, singing along to a CD of Christian songs, some of Deborah's favorites . . . The moment Michael stepped through the door, the song "We Are Standing on Holy Ground" began to play: "We are standing on holy ground, and I know that there are angels all around."

As the song washed through the room, Michael looked at Deborah, then at Mary Ellen. "We are on holy ground," he whispered. Then as though someone had kicked the backs of his legs, he fell to his knees and wept.

In early 2009, my partner, Michael Altman, gave a copy of *Same Kind of Different as Me* to Howard Godel, another prominent New York art dealer, who read it and passed it along to his wife, Melinda. The couple had a friend, Erin Cortright, who could relate to Deborah's story better than most.

In August 2008, at the age of fifty-two, Erin found herself inexplicably short of breath. She went to see an internist, who x-rayed her chest, pronounced her lungs clear, and sent her home with an inhaler. But a few weeks later, while hiking the hills amid the bell towers of Tuscany with Nate, her husband of twenty-two years, Erin felt a weakness she had never known.

In the middle of a dirt road alongside a sun-drenched vineyard, she stopped and looked at Nate. "Something's wrong with me."

Back in the States, the diagnosis was not good. Erin had acute myelogenous leukemia (AML), a rare form of the disease for which there is no known cure.

In October, Erin checked into a hospital for a series of chemotherapy treatments. Doctors had told her that chemo is effective in a small number of AML cases. In Erin's case, it wasn't. In January

2009, doctors transferred to her to Calvary Hospital, a hospice facility where she would wait to die.

"When I first got there, I was really sick," she remembers. "There was one night when I had multiple infections, a 104-degree temperature, and internal bleeding. I didn't know if I was going to make it."

The hospice doctor and chaplain told Erin's husband to make sure her affairs were in order and to tell anyone who wanted to say good-bye that they should do so that night.

But Erin kept on living.

Two months later, during a visit in March, Howard and Melinda Godel gave Erin a copy of our book. Erin read of Deborah's strength, of her faith in the face of death. And Erin felt a kinship with Deborah. Like my wife, she wanted to see her son graduate from high school and college. She wanted to see him get married. She wanted to meet her grandchildren. But none of that was going to happen. Instead Erin was winding up her last days on earth, leaving behind a husband and son.

"Some might wonder how could someone in my position read a book like that?" Erin says. "Some might think it odd for someone to even give me a book like that. But I found it comforting. I could relate to it completely. I found it inspiring that Deborah put everyone else in her life first. I felt that if I met Deborah, her cup would never be half-empty but always half-full."

When she finished reading the book, Erin realized that there was actually a good chance she would meet Deborah—in heaven.

Though she had survived her brush with death in January, doctors assured her that nothing had changed. The chemo had failed, and the leukemia was still in charge. One doctor told Erin that AML patients typically live only two to four months after chemo failure.

"The night I finished the book, I remember praying that Deborah would be the first person I saw when I got to heaven," she says. "At the same time, I was concerned about my husband. He was going to be going on without me. I wanted to talk to Ron and see if he was okay, see how he was managing."

In April, when Melinda and Howard visited again, Erin told them how much she'd liked our book.

"We're going to see Ron Hall's partner at an art show tonight," Melinda said. "Maybe he can put you in touch with Ron."

And that's how it happened that, within a day or so, I had Erin Cortright on the phone.

I started off the conversation asking about her illness, how she was feeling, that sort of thing. Erin answered me politely but quickly fast-forwarded the conversation. "I don't want this call to be about me," she said. "I know what's going to happen to me, and I've accepted that. I'm at peace with it. Now I want to talk about you and Denver. I want you to tell me everything you've done since Deborah left earth and went to heaven because I'm going to be going there soon, and when I get there, I want to tell her everything!"

I have no idea whether our loved ones watch us from heaven,

keeping up with our earthly lives the way some folks keep up with their daily soaps. Since the Scripture says that in heaven there are no more tears, I tend to think the souls up there can't see the people down here. I don't see how they could watch our tragedies unfold and not cry over them. Wouldn't it be wonderful if they could only see the good parts?

Holding the phone, I sat in my bedroom at the Murchison estate, looking at a credenza filled with framed photographs that seemed sharply divided into two eras—With Deborah and Since Deborah. There were pictures of Deborah with Carson, Deborah with Regan, Deborah and me posing at some resort or another, having had no idea when the picture was snapped that soon death would draw a line across time.

So even though I didn't know for sure, I liked the idea that in Erin I now had a link to what Denver calls "the other side." A messenger who was not only willing but also *eager* to get there and fill my wife in on whatever she might have missed.

"I want to know about Denver," Erin said first. "Are you two still friends?"

I chuckled in an "if you only knew" kind of way. "Yes, we're still friends, still roommates, traveling all over the country, telling Deborah's story. Tell her I didn't catch and release him!"

"And the mission," Erin said. "What's it like now? Is it everything Deborah dreamed of?"

An unexpected flash of pleasure warmed my veins as I remembered our first trip to East Lancaster and the vision Deborah had.

I had pulled into the mission parking lot, wondering how quickly I'd be able to pull out again, but Deborah suddenly spoke in a tone that you learn to recognize when you've loved someone for years, a tone that says, "Hear me on this."

"Ron, before we go in, I want to tell you something." She leaned back against her headrest, closed her eyes. "I picture this place differently than it is now. White flowerboxes lining the streets, trees and yellow flowers. Lots of yellow flowers like the pastures at Rocky Top in June."

Deborah opened her eyes and turned to me with an expectant smile "Can't you just see that? No vagrants, no trash in the gutters, just a beautiful place where these people can know that God loves them as much as He loves the people on the other side of that tunnel."

I smiled, kissed my fingertips, and laid them against her cheek. "Yes, I can see that." And I could. I just didn't mention that I thought she was getting a little ahead of herself.

As usual, I was wrong. When Deborah and I first visited, I told Erin, we entered a rundown building filled with good-hearted people like mission director Don Shisler and Chef Jim. People who faithfully ministered to the homeless, doing the hard work of rescuing lost souls, making do with what God had provided to that point. Chef Jim died of cancer before he could see the memorial chapel that bears Deborah's name, the new men's center, women's center, and free medical clinic.

The clinic has revolutionized care at the mission because it includes a mental-health division. As Denver mentioned earlier, Don estimates that up to 70 percent of homeless people suffer from varying degrees of mental-health issues. Before the clinic, the Union Gospel Mission lacked the capacity to offer these folks any meaningful on-site help. Now volunteer counselors and psychologists can intervene directly and also refer those with chronic mental conditions to agencies that can get them on the path to healing.

The clinic was spearheaded by Dr. Alan Davenport. Alan and his wife, Mary Ellen, were our closest family friends and, throughout Deborah's illness, our staunchest supporters.

"You probably remember reading about them in the book," I said to Erin.

She said that she did. Then, like a reporter with a fast-approaching deadline, she popped her next question. "What about Sister Bettie? I just loved her in the book. How's she doing?"

I met Sister Bettie before I met Miss Debbie. She ain't no nun or nothin like that. We call her "Sister" 'cause she's a real spiritual woman . . . When she's talkin to you, she'll lay a hand on your arm like she's knowed you all your life, like maybe you was her own child . . .

Sister Bettie lives at the mission, but it ain't 'cause she don't have nowhere else to go. A long time ago, she lived in a regular neighborhood. But after her husband died, Sister

Bettie felt the Lord tuggin on her heart, tellin her to spend the rest a' her life servin the homeless. She sold her home and everything she had except for a little bitty Toyota truck, and she asked the folks at the Union Gospel Mission could she set up housekeepin down there.

It didn't take long 'fore most a' the homeless folks in Fort Worth knowed Sister Bettie. She'd go to restaurants to ask em for their leftovers, and stores to ask em for socks and blankets and toothpaste and such . . . She never carried no purse with her, just whatever she had to give out that day and her Bible.

"Sister Bettie's perking along just as sweet as ever," I told Erin. "She still calls me all the time. She still prays with me about Deborah." Well along into her eighties, Sister Bettie still hauls her old bones out on the streets every week to love on some of the grubbiest people you will ever meet, smiling under her cloud of white hair, her blue eyes twinkling like sun on the sea.

Erin pressed on: "Did your kids get married?"

"Oh, yes," I said.

"Who did they marry? Will Deborah know them when I tell her?"

Deborah would know Carson's wife, Megan, I said. Before she died, Deborah had hoped Carson would marry Megan and had given Carson a strand of pearls for his bride to wear on their wedding day.

As for Regan, Deborah always worried about her attraction

to vagabond nonconformists and was sure Regan would wind up marrying some hippie snowboarder from Vail who wore his cap backward and worked in a T-shirt shop. Instead, I told Erin, Regan had followed in her mother's footsteps and married an investment banker. Except that Regan's pick, Matt Donnell, came from a West Texas ranching family instead of the smelly side of the tracks in Haltom City.

"Tell Deborah that Regan and Matt have two daughters," I said to Erin. "Griffin is three, and Sadie Jane is a year old."

"What about Carson and Megan? Do they have kids?"

My heart caught in my chest. "Yes, they have one child, a daughter."

I flashed back to the day she was born. When I walked into the hospital room, Carson placed a tiny bundle in my arms. I looked down at her tiny features—eyes closed; lips a faint whisper of pink; sweet, round head covered with the barest breath of hair, like the soft surface of a peach.

"Dad," Carson said, "welcome the newest Deborah Hall to the world—Kendall Deborah Hall."

I stood there and cried and wished my wife could be the one to hold her namesake.

But now, at least, Erin could pass on the good news about all Deborah's granddaughters . . . and about the fulfillment of so many of her dreams. Dreams for our family, yes. Dreams for Denver and for the mission she cared so much about.

My wife had foreseen that Denver, a man the world would

call foolish, would be wise enough to change a city, Fort Worth—and he did. She had predicted that Denver and I would be friends—and we were. But not even Deborah could have foreseen all the amazing ways that God has used our experiences to change people's hearts toward the homeless across the country and around the world.

Wrapping up another miraculous phone call generated by Deborah's story, Erin said, "Is there anything else you want me to tell Deborah when I see her in heaven?"

"Yes," I said. "Tell her Ronnie Ray says hello, that I miss her, and that I'll see her soon."

About the Authors

Ron Hall is an international art dealer whose long list of regular clients includes many celebrity personalities. An MBA graduate of Texas Christian University, he divides his time between Dallas and his Brazos River ranch near Fort Worth.

Denver Moore currently serves as a volunteer at the Fort Worth Union Gospel Mission. He lives in Dallas, Texas.

Lynn Vincent is the author or coauthor of seven books and a senior writer for *WORLD* magazine, where she covers politics, culture, and current events. She lives in San Diego, California.

Follow Ron and Denver on Twitter.com/RonandDenver. Keep up with the latest news on their travels and speaking engagements as well as bits of Denver's wisdom and progress being made for an upcoming movie.

It begins outside a burning plantation hut in Louisiana . . . and an East Texas honky-tonk . . . and, without a doubt, in the heart of God. It unfolds in a Hollywood hacienda . . . an upscale New York gallery . . . a downtown dumpster . . . a Texas ranch.

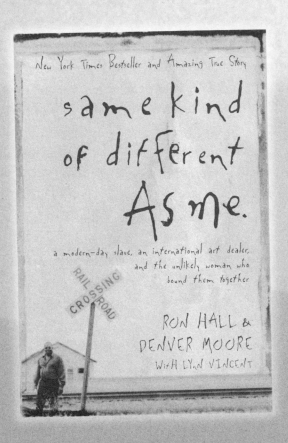

New York Times Bestseller and Amazing True Story

same kind of different As me.

a modern-day slave, an international art dealer, and the unlikely woman who bound them together

RON HALL & DENVER MOORE

WITH LYNN VINCENT

978-0-8499-0041-9

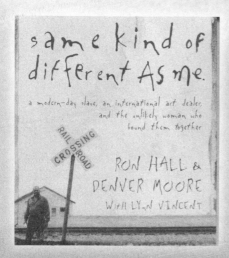

Go Deeper into the Heart-Tugging Story

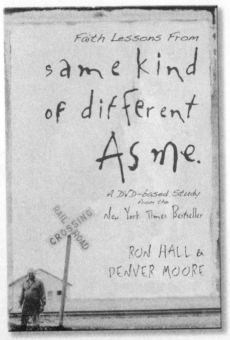

978-1-4185-4286-3

Perfect for your individual study or small-group discussion, *Faith Lessons from… Same Kind of Different as Me DVD-Based Study* provides an eye-opening account of 20th century slavery in the US, continued connection to the story of life-changing friendship, and foundation for a convicting lesson.

This documentary-style video, along with the Participant's Guide (978-1-4185-4287-0), brings themes from the *New York Times* Best-Selling trade book to life. To learn more visit *www.ThomasNelson.com*.